To

_____

From

_____

Date

_____

*For the hurt of the daughter of my people
I am hurt. I am mourning; Astonishment
has taken hold of me. Is there no balm in
Gilead, Is there no physician there? Why
then is there no recovery for the
health of the daughter of my people?*

Jeremiah 8:21-22

Healing of the Female Spirit

Unless otherwise indicated, all scriptural references are from the *King James Version* of the Bible.

Verses marked The Message are taken from *The Message*. Copyright © 1993, 1994, 1995, 1996, 2000, 2001, 2002. Used by permission of NavPress Publishing Group.

Verses marked NKJV are taken from the *New King James Version*. Copyright © 1982 by Thomas Nelson, Inc. Used by permission. All rights reserved.

Verses marked NLT are taken from the *Holy Bible, New Living Translation*, copyright © 1996. Used by permission of Tyndale House Publishers, Inc., Wheaton, Illinois 60189. All rights reserved.

Verses marked KNOX are taken from *The Word: The Bible from 26 Translations*, ISBN 0935491015, © 1991-2004. Mathis Publishers, Inc., Gulfport, MS 39506

Verses marked NRSV are taken from the *New Revised Standard Version Bible*, copyright 1989, Division of Christian Education of the National Council of the Churches of Christ in the United States of America. Used by permission. All rights reserved.

For emphasis, the author has placed selected words from Bible quotations in italics and/or parenthesis.

Healing of the Female Spirit
Published by: Media Group™
www.globalrevival.com

Copyright © 2004 Dr. Robin Harfouche. All rights reserved. Reproduction of text in whole or part without the express written consent by the author is not permitted and is unlawful according to the 1976 United States Copyright Act. Printed in the United States of America.

DR. ROBIN HARFOUCHE

Healing of the Female Spirit

Dedication

*This book is dedicated
to all women everywhere.*

Acknowledgements

*I just want to thank,
with all my heart and all my love,
Christine Loretz and Robert Brady
for their incredible work on this project.
Our goal is, as always,
"It's All About Souls."
It's nice to have people with you
who are willing to pay the price.*

Table of Contents

Foreword	....	1
Introduction	....	3
Chapter One	The Sword of the Spirit...........	7
	Your Spiritual Makeup...........	11
	Spirit Facts...........................	12
	Who Am I?.............................	14
	Opened unto God....................	16
Chapter Two	Life in the Creative Moment....	21
	Innocence Lost.......................	23
	Ties to the Past......................	26
	Violation................................	28

	Living Life and Loving It……...	30
Chapter Three	Woman, Where Are Your Accusers?...............................	35
	Wading through Opposition….	40
	That Thing Called Intuition…..	42
	And God Gave Gifts to Men….	44
	Protecting the Gift……………	46
	Mini Skirts and High Spiked Heels………………………….	48
	Team Ministry……………..…	50
Chapter Four	Accelerated Growth in God….	55
	Releasing the Gift……….…...	57
	Giving Birth to Your Destiny...	60
	Channeling God's Power……..	63

	Enjoying the View...............	64
	Making Room for the Gift......	66
	Women with Purpose...........	69
Chapter Five	Recognizing Your Protector....	73
	Embraced by Love Himself.....	78
	Women of God...................	79
	The Spirit of Lust................	81
	Loved into Freedom.............	83
Chapter Six	Free from Shame................	87
	Created for Love.................	91
	Healing in Gilead.................	94
	The Daughters of God...........	96

	Forgiveness............................	98
	It's *That* Easy..........................	100
Chapter Seven	Self-Preservation...................	105
	Sparkling Clean...................	107
	Jesus Invented Sex...............	109
Chapter Eight	Leave My Women Alone!.......	113
	Love Covers.......................	116
	Covered by the Blood............	118
Chapter Nine	Secrets to a Great Marriage.....	123
	Spirit-Mates.......................	125
	The Strongest Spiritual Weapon..	127

	Soul Ties..............................	129
	The Truth about Physical Manifestations.........................	132
	Tried By the Light...…............	134
	Closing the Door..............…..……	135
Chapter Ten	Beyond Brokenness…......…..	139
	When Life Lost Its Color….......	141
	Searching for Purpose............	143
	Freak Accident.......................	146
	Destiny Calling..................…..	149
	Coating through Hollywood.…	151
	Encounter with God…............	153
	Hello, This is God…................	155
	Appointment with Power…......	157

	Now is Your Time...............	159
Chapter Eleven	Astounding Miracles............	165
	Miracles on the Frontier.........	168
	Divine Initiative...................	172
	Dealing with Healing.............	176
	The Working of Miracles.......	178
	Naturally Supernatural...........	182
	Everything Danced.................	183
Chapter Twelve	Visions and Revelations.........	189
	Stolen Miracle....................	193
	City in the Sky....................	195
	The Sound of Heaven.............	198

	The Miracle Move of God......	200
	The Spirit of Pain.................	201
	Vendetta against Darkness......	203
Chapter Thirteen	Impregnated by Desire..........	207
	The Substance of God...........	213
	Be It unto Me, God..............	215
	The Crown of Glory................	218
Epilogue	Reach for the Stars...............	221
	The Healing Continues..........	224
	Mobilizing the Army of God...	227
	Spirit Training.....................	229
	Every Increasing Glory.........	231

Foreword

I am eighteen years old and I am the *most confident woman you'll ever meet*. I am genuinely *happy to be me*! Oh yes, I'm sure some people wish that I wasn't as comfortable with my loud, blunt, *black and white, never stop 'till I get what I want* personality. They can wish all they want, but I won't ever change. I am confident being me. I know *exactly* who I am and who God wants me to be.

Like most women, I am a very complicated individual. As much as I am strong, I am sensitive. As much as I am self-sufficient, I am needy.

My mom, Dr. Robin, has had more to do with my character development than she knows! Through all the teenage hormones and the peer pressure, she has guided me. She has led me by the Word of God through the minutest of irritations. Mom nurtures my *passionate personality*. She doesn't squelch it, like some people have tried to do.

The principles that she will teach you in *Healing of the Female Spirit* are the *same principles* that have made me who I am today. You, through this book, will become the woman that you've always wanted to be, but never dreamed possible. Insecurity and fear will no longer hold you back and you will not be confined to a religious box. You will be exactly *who* God wants you to be. You will be fearlessly *free*.

Welcome to my personal *Mother-Daughter* talks!

Christie "Amira" Harfouche

Introduction

Dear Child of God,

This is it. This is your time to be free. Heaven has been preparing *you* for this moment.

God has a *specific* miracle for you. It may be a physical miracle. It may be a spiritual miracle. It may be an emotional miracle. It may be a deliverance miracle. You may have a combination of several miracle needs. Perhaps, nobody has really heard you, but God has heard your cry. He knows your needs. He knows your thoughts. He knows what your heart is prepared for.

Somewhere deep inside you said to God, *"Oh, I want to be healed…I want to be free…I want this thing to stop…I want it to leave me alone…I want to be forever changed."*

Right now, you have an appointment with destiny. The book that you are holding in your hands is not merely the product of paper and ink, but it contains the supernatural prescription to bring you into the wholeness that you have longed for. In the realm of the Spirit, God has prepared you for this time. He has sent His gifts from heaven to heal your heart. If you could see into the realm of the Spirit, you would know that breakthrough *is as close as your next breath*. In the coming pages, God will supernaturally prepare your heart for healing and restoration. Get ready. This is your time of healing.

Dr. Robin Harfouche

*You can hear something once
under the inspiration of the Holy Spirit,
and that Word will pierce into your heart
through the love of God, and accomplish
in that very second what God has sent it to do.*

Chapter 1

The Sword of the Spirit

The healing of the female spirit is one of the most important things that women need in the world today. As we prepare to go into that place of healing, I'd like to show you how the Word of God and the Holy Spirit will bring about this change in your life.

> **For the Word of God is quick, and powerful, and sharper than any two edged sword, piercing even to the dividing asunder of soul and spirit,**

and of the joints and marrow, and is a discerner of the thoughts and intents of the heart.

Hebrews 4:12

The Word of God is alive and powerful. Jesus is the Word made flesh. Therefore, the very essence of the Word is spirit and life. As you are reading this under the inspiration of the Holy Spirit, the sword of the Spirit is actively working in your life. It is working to accomplish what it was sent out to do. It will not return void. It will produce results. Jesus will heal your heart and the provision of heaven will bring restoration to your soul.

The Word of God is active and effective in your life. The Word of God is active and effective in your life.

The Word of God is sharp. In fact, it's sharper than *any* two-edged sword! You don't have to hit someone over the head with it or hack them up with it. It's not that kind of a sword! It is not a dull sword that renders repeated blows. In other words, you can hear something *once* under the inspiration of the Holy Spirit, and that Word will pierce into your heart through the love of God and accomplish in that very second what God has sent it to do. Isn't that good news?

The Word of God is sharper than any two-edged sword *piercing*....

Another word for *piercing* is **penetrating**. The Word of God is penetrating. As you read this, the Word of God is penetrating into different areas of your life. You may not even know all the areas that the Word of God needs to penetrate! You may have a conscious understanding of some of those areas, but the Word of God *has an intimate knowledge* of the areas that He needs to perform a deep healing in.

...even to the dividing asunder of *soul* and *spirit*, and of the joints and marrow....

The Word of God accurately divides between the soul and the spirit and the joints and the marrow. Do you know the reason that the Lord gives that example? Medical doctors tell us that it is *impossible* to divide the joint from the marrow of the bone. It is physically impossible! There is no knife that exists – there is no laser surgery – there is no way that you can separate the joint from the marrow. When God used that analogy, He wanted to show you how powerful and how accurate the Word of God is, even compared to the best surgeon's scalpel.

> *The sword of the Spirit will penetrate, reveal, and heal.*

Jesus – the Word of God – is the revelation of the love of God on the planet. That love and the very Word of His power will access every area of your being. The sword of the Spirit will penetrate, reveal, and heal the most intimate areas of your heart.

Your Spiritual Makeup

Your *soul* is comprised of your **mind**, **will** and **emotions**. Defined by experience or knowledge, your soul is the seat of your mental faculties. It's your personal world view. It's *how* you feel and *why* you feel a particular way. Since the fall, humankind has used signals from the soul to survive. It has acted as the *governing factor* within the unregenerate human experience.

Your spirit is absolutely **perfect**. Your spirit is the recreated, beautiful, born again part of you – the inner man. Before you received salvation, your human spirit was dead and bound under the curse of the law. When you received Jesus Christ as your Savior, your human spirit *instantaneously* became born again. It became new. At that moment, you received access to the mind of Christ and the ability to once again rule over the soul and the body. (1 Corinthians 2:16)

> *Your spirit is the recreated, beautiful, born again part of you.*

Spirit Facts

Y**ou are a spirit, you have a soul, and you live in a body.** You are *not* a walking brain. *You are a spirit.* Your born again spirit has been recreated according to God. It has been designed to rule or govern over every other part of your makeup. This doesn't happen automatically. Your physical body and your soul (mind, will and emotions) need to be retrained according to the Word of God.

> **And be not conformed to this world: but be ye transformed by the renewing of your mind…**
>
> Romans 12:2a

The Child of God is instructed to renew their natural minds to the Word of God. A natural mind that is renewed has the ability to operate in the mind of Christ. They have trained their soul to maintain agreement with the frequency of heaven.

The Child of God who has *not* renewed their mind in a certain area, senses the world through the soul realm. They are governed by their five senses, not by the mind of Christ. They live from *feeling to feeling,* realigning their world view to fit their human experience. They are not governed by their recreated spirit. Why is this important?

I want you to understand how God created you and what part of your makeup needs a healing. You see, your body or your emotions may need a healing, but then the Word of God may penetrate into an area of your life and reveal a part of your will that needs to come in line with the Word of God.

> *You are a spirit, you have a soul, and you live in a body.*

The desire of heaven is for you to experience a complete healing in your life. God wants you to be whole, *spirit, soul* and *body*. In the coming chapters, you will receive a divine deposit. The light of revelation will dawn in your heart, and restoration will come to your total being.

Who Am I?

...and is a discerner of the thoughts and intents of the heart.

The Word of God is a discerner of the thoughts and the intents of your heart. Another way to describe the intent of the heart is **your moral understanding**. Your moral understanding is how you perceive the world and how you understand life based on your frame of reference. Your frame of reference is either your experiential knowledge or your understanding of the Word of God.

A Child of God must train their reasoning faculties.

Why does that make a difference?

The Word of God will reveal things to you that have adversely affected your understanding of the world. Past experiences, hurts, and wounds may subconsciously thrust a person back into repeated patterns of defeat. The glass ceiling of experience can prevent a Child of God from participating in the God kind of life. These are things that you might not even know about, but they are holding you back from being the best woman that you could be in Jesus. Your moral understanding has to be reshaped and redefined by the Word of God. This happens through revelation. A Child of God must train their reasoning faculties to stand in agreement with their born again spirit.

Opened unto God

Neither is there any creature that is not manifest in his sight: but all things are naked and opened unto the eyes of him with whom we have to do.

Hebrews 4:13

In the eyes of God, you are *naked* and *opened* before Him. It's **o-p-e-n-*e-d***. I want you to see that *opened* is past tense. You have been opened like a box is opened. You've been opened by Jesus Christ — by the Word of God. Are you ready for something that is just going to rock you? The word *opened* in the original language means to expose the gullet of a victim for killing. It also means to seize by the throat or the neck.

There is nothing in you that is hidden from God's sight.

Am I saying that God is going to seize you? No! I'm saying that there is *nothing* in you that is hidden from God's sight. All things are opened! Baggage? What about those *things* that generate feelings of inferiority and cause you to hate what you see in the mirror? They're opened before the sight of God! What about those *things* that cause you to put up with abusive situations? They're exposed! What about the *thing* that robs you of the ability to love? All of those things are made manifest and are opened! God, the Holy Ghost, has a hold of the jugular vein of whatever it is in your life that is holding you back. Right now, He is ready to penetrate that thing by the Word of His power. I like to say it like this, "Once it is revealed, it's too late devil – it's healed!"

Insecurity doesn't allow you to live in the now, but causes you to always think backward.

Chapter 2

Life in the Creative Moment

Have you ever walked away from a conversation and said, "*What* did I just say and *why* did I just say that?" You leave the conversation and then replay it a thousand times, wondering, "What did they think of me? Why don't I just be quiet?"

What is happening?

That is insecurity plaguing you! Insecurity doesn't allow you to *live in the now* but causes you to always think *backward* – about what you did, about what you said yesterday. You're always reviewing yourself, unable to go forward and live in the creative moment.

The creative moment is a now moment, full of freedom of expression and spontaneity.

The creative moment is a *now moment*, full of freedom of expression and spontaneity. You've seen children do it! In a moment, a child will rip off their clothes and run out in the middle of a field. There they are – *free* and living in the creative moment!

Why do human beings grow up out of that free flow of creativity? What happened? What happened to the carefree spontaneity that a child embraces? What caused them to draw back from the expression of life?

Innocence Lost

Therefore shall a man leave his father and his mother, and shall cleave unto his wife: and they shall be *one flesh*. And they were both naked, the man and his wife, and were *not ashamed*.

Genesis 2: 24-25

This is a familiar portion of scripture, but stay with me because you're going to see it differently today. I want you to see that they were *naked* and *not ashamed*.

***Now the serpent* was the shrewdest of all the creatures the LORD God had made. "Really?" he asked the woman. "Did God really say you must not eat any of the fruit in the garden?"**

Genesis 3:1 NLT

Let's look at the first three words of Genesis 3:1 again: ***now the serpent***. They were naked, and they were not ashamed *until* the serpent gained access into their lives. Innocence lost.

> **There's more to sex than mere skin on skin. Sex is as much spiritual mystery as physical fact. As written in Scripture, "The two become one." Since we want to become spiritually one with the Master, we must not pursue the kind of sex that avoids commitment and intimacy, leaving us more lonely than ever - the kind of sex that can never "become one." There is a sense in which sexual sins are different from all others. In sexual sin we violate the sacredness of our own bodies, these bodies that were made for God-given and God-modeled love, for "becoming one" with another. Or didn't you realize that your body is a sacred place, the place of the Holy Spirit? Don't you see that you can't live however you please, squandering what God paid such a high price for? The physical part of you is not some piece of property belonging to the spiritual part of you. God owns the whole works. So let people see God in and through your body.**
>
> 1 Corinthians 6:16-20 The Message

Therefore a man leaves his father and mother and embraces his wife. They become one flesh.

Genesis 2:24 The Message

Why did it talk about *one flesh*? Let's discuss innocence lost. If you are not a virgin, I would like you to remember where you lost it. Close your eyes, and just remember. I was born in 1957, and in those days I think the backseat of a car was used a lot. My mother had four children before she was twenty. She had her first child at fifteen. Do you remember now?

Do you understand why it is termed, *"lost your virginity?"* *"Lost"* - it wasn't *"gave* my virginity." It should be "gave." When a boy and girl who know Jesus get married (and they are both pure), they are not ashamed of being naked! They don't know sin. They don't have baggage to clean up. When they are making love, they don't call each other by the wrong name!

Ties to the Past

Do you remember when you had your first sexual feeling? Was it a clean, sanctified feeling or were you ashamed of it? What happened as a result of that encounter? The Word of God clearly indicates that when you "lose" it, you become *one flesh*. Why are you having emotional problems? Perhaps, you haven't gotten over the *one flesh* that is in your past. For many people, it was more than one. The Bible says that if you join yourself to another, you become *one flesh*. That means there is an open door in the realm of the spirit. There is an actual tie between you and that other person. That tie needs to be severed with the sword of the Spirit.

> *The Bible says that if you join yourself to another, you become one flesh.*

If you are married and your marriage bed is undefiled, are there still things coming into that marriage bed from the past? Do you experience condemnation every time you have a sexual feeling? When you look in the mirror, do you see the glory of God or do you hear thoughts of condemnation and torment? When you are alone, do you have sexual feelings that suddenly come upon you from out of nowhere? Women ask me, "I am married now to a good man, but when I am with him, I have thoughts. I don't understand those thoughts because my bed is sanctified. Where are these thoughts coming from? I don't feel free to express myself."

> *When you look in the mirror do you see the glory of God?*

Those things shouldn't be touching you! They are all leftovers from the *one body*. We are dealing with healing of the female spirit. Jesus by His Spirit, by the precision of the sword of the Spirit, is going to cut those ties from your past! *What is revealed, is healed.*

Violation

I don't remember the first time I was sexually violated. I was too young, but I do remember responding. Somebody said, "Oh that's terrible!" No, I remember feeling sexual at four and five years old. I used to pretend I was asleep. In my mind, I used to go and hide in a little black box. I would hide myself away while that physical violence was being done to my body.

I felt guilt all of my life, even into my beautiful marriage. I didn't know it was there. Deep down, I felt like I had somehow brought that thing on. Perhaps that little girl had seduced that old man?

> *I felt guilt all of my life, even into my beautiful marriage.*

After my marriage, every time that I wanted to react physically in a sanctified way, those old feelings would come up again. I never felt clean because there were *one body ties* that needed to be broken. Those ties needed to be dealt with in the realm of the Spirit. I would tell my husband, "Sweetheart, I am going through the motions right now. I can't *just* be physical. I am spirit, soul and body. There is a part of me that is going through some kind of torment right now. Let's talk about it." Thank God that I was married to a beautiful man of God who would let me stop and help me through it. One time, for eight hours, the Lord took me back in my memory. He showed me times when I had been sexually violated and how those times had bound me and left doors open to my emotional makeup. Those open doors triggered relentless feelings of condemnation and torment.

> *In God, there are no feelings of condemnation or guilt.*

Some of you were violated; that's how you lost your innocence. Others gave it to the best looking guy in high school, but you still lost it. Others kept it until you got married. That's awesome! In God, there are no feelings of condemnation, guilt, or any type of pornographic feelings. None of those feelings are supposed to be attached to your sexuality in God. If they are, it's because there are doors left open.

Living Life and Loving It!

Do you want to breathe the exhilaration of freedom? Do you want to radiate with the love of God? Do you want to be filled and energized with courage, triumphant boldness, strength and supernatural sobriety? Do you want to be so free, so healed from the past, that you respond to life according to your recreated spirit nature?

The Word of God is going into your heart to extract the old and heal what was broken. As you yield to this, you will overflow with the life of God until the anointing exudes out of every pore of your being. You will be so healed and so full of the pure power of God that when you walk into an elevator, people will fall out under the power because of the anointing. You are a *healed vessel,* and the glory of God will flow out of you uninhibited by the things of the past. The anointing and the wisdom of God will run through your mind. You won't walk around in confusion. The absence of confusion will yield to the peace of God. Peace will reign in your heart. You will lift your hands, and ask for the wisdom of God, and the wisdom will be there. *Just like that*, you will be the

> *The glory of God will flow out of you uninhibited by the things of the past.*

woman that has a word in season. You will have the right word at the right time. You will be on time in God! You can do that! Prepare your heart; this is your time of healing. The power of God is here to set you free.

If God has told you to be a corporate executive, do it. Don't be intimidated! Walk into the board room after you've prayed, "Shaka Shaka!" and say, "Back up boys! God gave me a divine idea!"

Chapter 3

Woman, Where Are Your Accusers?

Just then a woman of the village, the town harlot, having learned that Jesus was a guest in the home of the Pharisee, came with a bottle of very expensive perfume and stood at his feet, weeping, raining tears on his feet. Letting down her hair, she dried his feet, kissed them, and anointed them with the perfume. When the Pharisee who had invited him saw this, he said to himself, "If this man was the prophet I

thought he was, he would have known what kind of woman this is who is falling all over him."

Luke 7:37-39 The Message

The Bible says that the Pharisee "said to himself." He didn't speak it out loud, but he was sitting there watching this woman who had come into his house. He knew what "kind of woman" she was. I don't know how he knew she was a sinner. Maybe she had braided hair or perhaps she wore gold necklaces? It's not clear exactly *how* the Pharisee knew, but he seemed to have some strong convictions about this woman. The woman also *seemed to know* exactly where his house was.

> *Jesus is the most touchable person in the universe.*

And Jesus answering said unto him…

Luke 7: 40a

Now look at that! The Pharisee didn't say anything out loud, but Jesus observed his heart. He also *observed the woman's heart*. This woman walked in, wept on the feet of Jesus, dried His feet with her hair and then anointed His feet with precious ointment. What did Jesus do? He just sat there. God in the flesh let a sinner touch Him. Jesus is the most touchable person in the universe.

And Jesus answered and said to him, "Simon,

I have something to say to you." So he said, "Teacher, say it." "There was a certain creditor who had two debtors. One owed five hundred denarii, and the other fifty. And when they had nothing with which to repay, he freely forgave them both. Tell Me, therefore, which of them will love him more?" Simon answered and said, "I suppose the one whom he forgave more." And He said to him, "You have rightly judged." Then He turned to the woman and said to Simon, "Do you see this woman? I entered your house; you gave Me no water for My feet, but she has washed My feet with her tears and wiped them with the hair of her head. You gave Me no kiss, but this woman has not ceased to kiss My feet since the time I came in. You did not anoint My head with oil, but this woman has anointed My feet with fragrant oil. Therefore I say to you, her sins, which are many, are forgiven, for she loved much. But to whom little is forgiven, the same loves little." Then He said to her, "Your sins are forgiven." And those who sat at the table with Him began to say to themselves, "Who is this who even forgives sins?" Then He said to the woman, "Your faith has saved you. Go in peace."

Luke 7:40-50 NKJV

What an account.

This woman basically walked in on a private dinner gathering. Refusing to be shut out, she intruded into the home of another. She did not have an invitation, but somehow she knew that the Master would not refuse her. With great preparation, she brought her offering. The host did not appreciate her presence or her gift of love. She was not invited. She was not welcome. She had violated all common protocol. The opinions of others paled in comparison to her desire to reach Jesus. Perhaps she had been blocked from Jesus before? Nevertheless, a supernatural boldness rose up within her and she knew that the Master would not condemn her nor her radical act of devotion.

> *She knew that the Master would not refuse her.*

It took *extreme boldness* for her to walk into that house. Have you ever shown up at a place where you were not invited? Your feelings will talk you right out the front door!

This woman did not go by what she felt. Most likely, all conversation ceased when she knelt at the feet of Jesus. With hot, tear-stained cheeks and a heavy heart, she gently kissed Her Master's feet. Silence hung heavy. As the eyes of the Pharisee bore into her, the air probably chilled over with disdain and disagreement. None of that dissuaded her. In her moment of vulnerability, she remained unmoved by the searing opinions of others. She didn't go by what she saw. She didn't go by what she felt. *She went directly for Jesus.*

Wading through Opposition

Sometimes you just have to wade through. You have to wade through what you're feeling, and you have to wade through the opinions of others. You have to press through that thing that would block you from the presence of God. As long as you are on this earth, you will face opposition. The temptation to draw back and recoil from life will never cease.

> *Your response to opposition will determine your height in God.*

Ultimately, your response to opposition will determine your height in God. There is a press involved. You have to press beyond the opinions of those who don't recognize the validity of your worship toward the Lord. Religious spirits are quick to judge and push you to the outside. If you go by what you feel, you will never enter in and touch the Lord. You will remain stagnant, never making headway in the things of God.

If the religious had their way, a prostitute would never get into the house of God. This is not about religion as an organization. This is about the religious spirits who persecuted Jesus Christ when He was on the earth. Those same religious spirits are still here! They didn't leave the planet when Jesus resurrected from the dead. They are still here today, influencing people and attacking women who desire to press into the fire of God.

That Thing Called Intuition

Let's talk about a woman's intuition. Before you met Christ, you lived life based on the input of your physical senses – your feelings. Women are the most sensitive creations on the planet. A man could walk into a room where everybody hates him, sit there, put his feet up on the desk and not even know that he is despised of all. A woman could walk into that same room and the hair will stand up on the back of her neck. She knows that something is definitely wrong!

> *Women are the most sensitive creations on the planet.*

Sometimes I think that men have it easier. Women were trained as little babies, "Oh, come and climb up on daddy's lap, honey. Cry it out, baby. Tell daddy how you feel." But not boys! "Suck it up, Jack! Don't be crying and slobbering! You're a man! You're twelve years old, suck it up!" Oh, but she's sixteen years old and she is daddy's little girl. She can go in there and have a sobbing session for hours and her father will help her! If his sixteen year old son Jerome comes in there and wants to cry, daddy will take him to the psychologist!

Women have been nurtured as sensitive creations! From

childhood, they learn that little girls are "sugar and spice and everything nice." Women are trained to *feel their way through life*. As a result, a woman will instinctively respond to her emotions. She will follow that *gut feeling*. That's called "a woman's intuition." A woman can walk into a room, and if somebody looks at her the wrong way, she will walk out and *never* come back again. She responds to her feelings.

> *A woman will clamp down on the call of God on her life to avoid being hurt.*

God has deposited gifts within each of His children. When a woman allows her gift or her talent to flow, she may feel vulnerable and naked. That gift is so precious! If anybody says the wrong thing to her, she may be tempted to instantly shut down! She may settle to avoid heartache. "Well I'll just help in the children's ministry, bless God. I don't need to be in the main sanctuary." A woman may clamp down on the call of God on her life to avoid being hurt.

And God Gave Gifts to Men

What do you do when God calls you and puts a gift on the inside of you? Do you sit on it, or do you allow it to make a way for you? God is calling women. There is nothing wrong with being an anointed housewife, if that is what God has called you to do. Personally, I hate cleaning. I hate cooking. If God has called you to do that, *then do it*. I love anointed housewives. If God has told you to be a corporate executive, *do it*. Don't be intimidated! Walk into the boardroom after you've prayed, *"SHAKA SHAKA SHAKA!"* and say, "Back up boys! God gave me a divine idea!"

> *What do you do when God calls you and puts a gift on the inside of you?*

My husband and I pastor together. I respect my husband with all my heart, but he pushes me! When I want to stay home and cry, he says, "Get out of that bed and pray in tongues!" There are times that I go to a meeting and get yelled up and down by some religious person who wants to rip me in shreds with their mouth. When I first started pastoring I would confess, "It's impossible to offend me!" I said that because everybody did! The temptation was there. This one particular lady came up to me one time and said, "You don't dress right for a pastor's wife." We pastor in the Southern part of the United States and I'm originally from California. Traditionally, the South is fairly conservative and religious. It's also known as the "Bible Belt." I said to her, "Well you know what, if you stay around long enough, God is going to deliver you of that religious spirit." She continued to sit under the Word, and she changed. Glory to God!

> *It's never personal. The warfare is over your call in God.*

They offended Christ, and they'll do it to you. They want to suck the life out of you and assault the gift. It's all about the anointing. It's all about the call. They want to shove your call down so far that you resign yourself to mere mortal existence.

If you're not answering the call of God that's on your life, then you're *existing*. You're not living. It's never personal. The warfare is over your call in God. It's all about purpose.

Protecting the Gift

Why do you need healing? Why do women need healing in their female spirit? It's the result of all the wounds. Women come into the Kingdom of God with baggage.

I remember the beginning of our ministry. My children were very little. I had two babies in a row because it needed to happen that way. We were traveling. We were fulfilling the call of God. We were preaching all over, living in motels and taking care of our babies.

> *Women come into the Kingdom of God with baggage.*

I remember pastor's wives living in their half-million dollar houses, and they would put my husband and me in the economy motel. After preaching, we would go back to the smoke-filled Motel 6 for a cup of coffee. I would put ice in the sink for the babies' milk bottles, and they went home to their comfort! The pastor's wives would sit me down and say, "How can you do this to your children?" I kept silent. Then I'd go back to my motel room and cry my eyes out. Was I doing something wrong? Maybe I should just stay home and let my husband go on the road by himself? Maybe I should just take care of those children? Believe me, it would have been easier!

You see, God called me to pay a price. He told me, "You didn't have the capacity to have those children." I was totally a mess in my female area from several abortions before I knew Christ. He said, "I gave you those children. If I gave you the call and I gave you the children, then I'm going to take care of both." He said, "Now you get up off of that bed, and quit feeling sorry for yourself." I'd go in the motel bathroom, shut the door, and pray my heart out in the Holy Ghost. *"HO SHAKA TAN DA LA SAN DA LA!"* I'd pray right past my mind. I'd pray right past my thinking. I'd pray right past the opinions of men, the opinions of women, the opinions of humanity, and the opinions of religious devils! I learned to protect the gift on the inside of me. Shutting my ears to the opposition and forsaking the opinions of others, I made the decision to press into the call of God.

> *I learned to protect the gift on the inside of me.*

Mini Skirts and High Spiked Heels

I never meant to be rebellious, but everybody thought I was just like that woman who broke into the Pharisee's house! When I first got saved, I walked around in a glory bubble. Thank God! I didn't know that everybody disapproved of me. I came to church wearing what I owned. I didn't have church dresses. I had mini skirts, high spiked heels, and bra-less t-shirts. I wanted to be in the presence of God more than anything! I just got dressed up and went to church. I didn't know! After awhile, I started noticing the disapproving glances of *"Sister Flowery-print-dress-and-a-doily-collar."* If you like doily collars, that's fine! Wear the doily collar and the big bow on the back of your head, but that's not my style!

> *When I first got saved, I walked around in a glory bubble.*

After enough of those disapproving looks, I thought, "If I just conform myself to what's acceptable, they will leave me alone." I looked at the typical *"preacher's wife,"* and I decided I would try to fit into that box. I thought, "Maybe if I look like them, they will leave me alone." Their words and their disapproving looks hurt my spirit. It was painful, so I tried. You should see the pictures. They are terrible! I used to be in the acting business and I felt like I was playing a part.

As long as I kept my mouth shut and my legs crossed, I didn't get any persecution. The moment I spoke, my facade was revealed. My mouth gave me away every time! I couldn't play the part. The Word was in my heart and in my mouth – like fire shut up in my bones! I couldn't relate to these people! Who are they? Is this the same Jesus that I met? Are they filled with fire? Are their bones rattling with the power of God? All they want to talk about is banana nut bread and Tupperware parties! All those things are important, but when I'm in the anointing, I want to talk about God! Iron sharpens iron. I want to talk about the revelation I just received. I want to talk about the power of God. I don't want to talk about the latest movie. I don't want to talk about who's sleeping with the latest Hollywood celebrity. I don't really care! I want to talk about God!

> *As long as I kept my mouth shut and my legs crossed, I didn't get persecution.*

Team Ministry

My husband and I pastor together. We are a team. Jesus called apostles, prophets, evangelists, pastors and teachers for the work of the ministry to build up the Saints. Five fold ministry gifts *include* females. There is no difference between male or female in the eyes of Jesus Christ. Jesus is female-friendly!

In the early days of our traveling ministry, we would get a lot of flack! We would go to a particular meeting and my husband would say, "My wife ministers with me." *"Your wife does what?"* "She ministers with me. We're a team. We minister together. My wife lays hands on the sick. My wife has words of knowledge. My wife has visions. My wife preaches. My wife ministers with me. Where I go, she goes."

> *Five fold ministry gifts include females!*

They would say, "Brother, you know, when the men leave the room, the women clean up the dishes. We all go in the other room and have a Cognac and smoke a cigar. You better leave the woman in the other room now." My husband would say, "She comes with me." He took the heat for my call! He stood up for me. He told people to leave me alone. He never told me what to wear. He never told me how to dress.

He did rebuke me when I got out of line, which was a lot. He would sit and listen to me minister. After the service, we would walk out and there would be complete silence. I wanted to hear, "*Wow!* Great message honey!" Instead, you could hear a pin drop. Oh, the silence! Finally I would work up the courage and ask the question, "So how did I do?" Then he'd explain to me. He would teach me. I would look over at him and say, "But that was God! I was in the anointing in there! Didn't you think I was anointed?" He'd say, "Yes, you were anointed, but it wasn't the Word of God."

> *My husband took the heat for my call.*

*You pray things out before you walk them out.
That's why it's so important that you
do not resist the Holy Ghost.
You need to pray out your tomorrow's, today.*

Chapter 4

Accelerated Growth in God

How did I grow? I studied the Word, and I prayed in the Holy Ghost *continually*. If you desire accelerated growth, you must press into accelerated obedience. Paul said, I pray in tongues *more than you all*. (1 Corinthians. 14:18)

Let me teach you. Don't run around in a frenzy, caught up with the cares of the world. Don't complain to your husband saying, "*Honey*, I need this. I need that." Just go to your prayer closet, and pray in your Holy Ghost language. Pray in tongues. Pray past your understanding.

Why don't you understand tongues? God gave you the gift of tongues because you don't have the capacity to deal with what you're saying. God prays His perfect will *through* you. You may be saying, "Make me bold! Make me aggressive. Help me to preach the Gospel. I want to do miracles. I want to cast out devils. I want to walk on water. I want to find gold in fishes' mouths!" Through the Holy Ghost, you are praying the perfect will of God for your life. You may be praying, "Get this man out of my life!" You don't even know it! You're dating, and you think he's the hottest thing you've ever seen. In the Holy Ghost you're praying, "He looks good on the outside, but he's not the right one. Deliver me Lord! Woooo! Glory!"

You can grow as fast as you're willing to flow in God.

How fast can you grow? You can grow as fast as you're willing to flow in God.

Releasing the Gift

The first time the Holy Ghost comes on you and your gift starts to move, you don't always do it right. There's not a book or a manual on how to move in the Holy Ghost. Flowing in the Spirit is just that, *flowing in the Spirit*. That means that you do whatever the Spirit says to do, whenever and however.

When I first got saved, everybody knew that I was the sinner! I looked like one with my racy, spiked heels! Everybody else looked saved and sanctified, wearing those doily collars. I would walk into a service and heads would jerk off their necks.

> *There's not a book or a manual on how to move in the Holy Ghost.*

In the beginning, I would always sit way in the back of the church because I didn't want to get prayed for. I knew that if I got prayed for, I would scream and hit the ground like a lightning bolt. It happened every time. Then everybody would say *"SINNER! SINNER! SINNER!"* When I was prayed for, the power of God would be on me so strong that my body would shake to the point of looking like I was shaking off of the floor.

I was radically saved and I was open. God just plugged me into the socket of His power. I was a willing vessel. Every morning I'd pray, "Jesus, if there is anything in me – if there is anything around me that will keep me from my destiny – *take it out*! I don't care what it feels like. Just take it out! I'm ready to change!" I prayed it every day, *so He did it every day*!

I remember the first time that I ever operated in tongues and interpretation. If you've never done it, you need to do it. You don't have to be a five-fold ministry gift to operate in tongues and interpretation. The power of God would come on me; my chest would be palpitating and beads of sweat would roll down my face. I didn't know what to do! All I knew was that there was a gigantic volcano getting ready to explode on the inside of me. If I didn't open my mouth, I was going to die! I was convinced that death was imminent! I didn't know when to open my mouth. I didn't know the appropriate time, but I *had* to open it. That's how God started using me at the beginning. I'd say, *"WOO WOOO, AH SHA LA LA DE LA LA."* I'd give a word in tongues. I didn't interpret it in English because that was way too scary. At least with tongues, you can't make a mistake. Nobody knows what you're saying, but the Holy Ghost knows how to pray.

> *As you put your natural with God's super, you will step into supernatural results in God.*

The minute you make a decision to yield to the flow of

the Holy Ghost, God will give you the divine ability to step out further than you've ever gone before. As you put your *natural* with God's *super*, you will step into *supernatural results* in God.

Giving Birth to Your Destiny

I prayed in tongues continually because my mind was absolutely useless! My mind would tell me the opposite of what the Word says. It was un-renewed and it would blare the sound of unbelief. I had to quiet it down so I could hear God. With practice, I realized that the only way to silence my thought life was to yell louder in a language that my brain couldn't comprehend. I would put my hands over my ears and pray, *"AH SHA LA LA DE LA!"* I'd pray like that and then all of a sudden I'd step over into another realm. I would shift into *travail*.

> *As you yield to the influence of the Spirit, you will go places in God.*

The Holy Ghost will pray through you. As you yield to the influence of the Spirit, you will go places in God. Travail is really different. It feels like you're going to explode from the inside out. There's a power on the inside of you that's being birthed into the earth realm. You can be lying on the floor, and you're groaning, *"AAAHHHH."* Tears are pouring out of your eyes, and your mind has no idea what's going on. I know it's a little weird. It's called praying under the inspiration of the Holy Ghost.

You pray things out before you walk them out. That's why it's so important that you do not resist the Holy Ghost. You need to pray out your tomorrow's, *today*.

When you pray in tongues, don't try to figure out what you're praying for! It can make you wiggy! You could be praying for Russia, for the call of God on your life, or for someone else. Unless the Lord gives you the interpretation, don't try to figure it out. Now, you can pray in tongues, flip over into English, and then flip back again into tongues.

> *You pray things out before you walk them out.*

You will go places in God in your prayer closet. You pray things out before you walk them out. I saw myself lay hands on the sick. I saw the blind eyes open. I saw cancer drop off people's bodies. I saw AIDS healed. I saw all of it in my prayer closet. I prayed it before I did it. I saw it, I prayed it, and then I did it.

Success is not just in your future. *Success is in your spirit.* Success is S*omeone* you're in partnership with right now. The only thing that is holding you back from fulfilling your God-given destiny is your lack of confidence in your dream. Go to your prayer closet, and yield to the inspiration of the Greater One that is on the inside of you. In the secret place, you will receive the boldness to hear God and to step out into the limitless expanse of faith. Go places with God. God wants to give you what you can't give yourself. Yield to the Holy Ghost. Pray it out. Let God design your life from the inside-out. Then you will have the supernatural empowerment to walk it out.

Channeling God's Power

If your soul is wounded, you can't be a pure channel of God's power. It will hinder the out-flow. God wants His power to rush through you like water gushing out from a fire hose. He wants *you* to be a conduit of His goodness.

The cleaner you are as a vessel, the more the power will rush through you. The less garbage, the less stuff stuck to the inside, the freer the power will be to flow through you uninhibited. As that power pours through you, it will loosen more stuff. When the power of God *loosens stuff*, it comes to the top. It surfaces. It manifests. *Once it's revealed, it's healed.*

> *If your soul is wounded, you can't be a pure channel of God's power.*

If there's an insecurity in your life, go to your prayer closet and yield to the Holy Ghost. Allow God's power to rush through your being and clean out what's not of Him. Go to your prayer closet and *worship Him*! Who cares what people think? This is between you and God! You do not need the approval of others to hit your prayer closet and travail until your call is birthed into the earth realm. You don't need anybody to approve of that!

Enjoying the View

Some of you will say, "You're not talking to me because I don't have a call." *That's not true!* The Bible says you are called. You may not be called to go out to the nations, but you are definitely called to walk a supernatural life. You are not called to walk like the world. You are called to walk from a heavenly perspective. You are the walking revelation of Jesus Christ on this planet. You are seated with Him in heavenly places. From your position, you are called to look down on the circumstances of life.

You know how little everything gets when you fly on an airplane? It gets little. The cities get little. People look like figurines. Swimming pools look like puddles. At that point, it doesn't matter what *Sister So-and-so* said. It doesn't matter what your bank account says. It doesn't matter what the bill collector says. You are up in the sky, and you are looking *down*. From that vantage point, *everything looks miniscule*. Things come into perspective. Jesus said we are seated with Him in heavenly places, far above principalities, powers, might and dominion. We are seated in Him. We have His heavenly perspective. We have a

> *You are the walking revelation of Jesus Christ on this planet.*

heavenly position. We have been given authority in Him over all the power of the devil. You have power to fly over everything that would assault the call of God on your life!

Making Room for the Gift

Why is the devil so afraid? Why is he so afraid of women? Do you know that fifty percent of the Body of Christ would be activated if women would just grab a hold of the call of God?

What do you think will happen if you're brimming with the power of God – full of love, compassion, mercy, grace, wisdom and the fruit of the Spirit? Do you know what's going to happen? You are going to have fewer of those raging hormonal imbalances! Let God work on you. It may take three or four years for somebody to recognize you, but the Word will work in your life. It worked in mine.

> *What do you think will happen if you're brimming with the power of God?*

I remember the first time that I met Dr. Lester Sumrall. Dr. Sumrall was eighty-three years old and had traveled to countless nations, written over one hundred books, had eleven television stations, and fed the hungry all over the world. He was an apostle. Everything in me anticipated his arrival. After devouring all of his books, I had such a tremendous respect for his gift. I knew God wanted to give me an impartation from the man of God.

Dr. Sumrall arrived, and I went with my husband to meet him in the car. He sat in the front seat and I sat in the back seat. When Dr. Sumrall got in the car, he wouldn't even look at me! He's from the old school – *the real old school*. I was devastated. He talked to my husband like he was a gem, a royal diadem – a precious diamond in his sight. He would say, "I just want to impart to you young man. You are Joshua. I am Moses. I want to impart to you." There I was in the back seat crying, "What about me?"

> *If I couldn't say anything good, I would just say it in tongues.*

After our first meeting, I went back to my house and prayed in tongues. I went to my prayer closet and made the decision not to complain. If I couldn't say anything good, I would just say it in tongues. If I started complaining, I would put my hand over my mouth and change my language. I went home and prayed, "Lord, why won't this man talk to me? I mean – I'm called! You told me I'm called!" God said to me, "He only recognizes the anointing." I said to God, "What do I do?" He said, "The next time you go to see him, *be prayed up*! You walk in there with the glory painted on you – you won't have to say anything."

The next day I walked in with the glory painted on me like a tabernacle. I just walked in. I was beaming. I had already prayed past the thing, and, if he didn't talk to me, I would be alright. I knew who I was and what I was called to do.

As I was sitting next to him, he looked up at me and just stared. Then he said, "You know, every fifty years God raises up one mighty woman." Oh, it didn't have to be me. It could have been any woman, but I was so happy that he talked to *me*! He said, "You can look back on it, every fifty years, one mighty miracle woman of God comes on the scene and just goes global." Then he stopped and started talking about something else. From that point forward, when he went to lay hands on my husband, his hand was on me too. I thought to myself, "Lord, it's true – a person's gift will make way for itself."

> *I knew who I was and what I was called to do.*

Women with Purpose

Sometimes I feel like grabbing women and shaking them. I just want to say, "Hello! You're filled with Jesus! Hello! Where's your gift? Hello!" Oh yes, I know that's not a very friendly thing to do. It may come off a little strong, but I want to grab them by the neck and say, "Wake up woman! Jesus is in the house! Wake up!"

Women say, "Well, I have no purpose." I'll give you one! I am telling you right now: I am on a mission with the King of Kings and the Lord of Lords! If you think purpose is all about getting up in the morning, cleaning your house and just being a good woman, then you're *not fulfilling your purpose*. Now is a time of destiny! God is calling out women who are willing to allow the Word of God to operate so strongly in them that they can minister to the needs of a hurting world. You can not give away what you do not have. You have to be full of your purpose!

> *You can not give away what you do not have.*

Why do you need to be one hundred percent of everything that God wants you to be? You need to be whole – not just for yourself – but for your sister, your auntie, your mother, or your children. You need to be whole for your sisters around the world who are suffering. You can open up your mouth with the power of God and give them the balm of Gilead. The Bible says, "He's in your heart and *He's in your mouth*." (Rom 10:8)

> *God is a great architect. Don't let the enemy lie to you about your worth.*

God is a great architect. Don't let the enemy lie to you about your worth. You are vitally important to God and His purpose on this planet. God has given you a specific job description. Only you can fulfill your call. Even now, you are being positioned for this final hour. You will fulfill your purpose, and your destiny will break forth like the sun. Woman of God, this is your time!

Put your hands on your spirit and say this:

"Jesus is in the House. This is the house. I am the house. I am the temple of God. God lives in me. I am righteous. I am holy. I am filled with peace. I am filled with joy. I am ready to go on. If there is anything in me that is hindering my purpose and my God-given destiny, take it out. Purpose is alive in me, and I am alive to purpose. I am ready to change! I am ready to go the distance. I am ready to yield to everything that God wants me to be. This is my time!"

*Every time you see Jesus,
you see women approaching Him.
He embraced them with a love and an
acceptance that they could not resist.*

Chapter 5

Recognizing Your Protector

Who is your defender? What is love? How does it feel? Right now, I would like you to touch His grace and His mercy in a way that you have never touched Him before. The love of God is tangible. God is love. Jesus is the Son of God – the love of God – sent for all humanity. He is the *express image* of God's person on this planet. Jesus set the example of how women should be treated. He is the perfect example of *how the Creator views you*.

> They say unto him, Master, this woman was taken in adultery, in the very act. Now Moses in the law commanded us, that such should be stoned: but what sayest thou? This they said, tempting him, that they might have to accuse him. But Jesus stooped down, and with his finger wrote on the ground, as though he heard them not. So when they continued asking him, he lifted up himself, and said unto them, He that is without sin among you, let him first cast a stone at her. And again he stooped down, and wrote on the ground. And they which heard it, being convicted by their own conscience, went out one by one, beginning at the eldest, even unto the last: and Jesus was left alone, and the woman standing in the midst.
>
> John 8:4-9

Who is your protector? What is love? Let's look at Jesus and how He responds to this beautiful lady.

> When Jesus had lifted up himself, and saw none but the woman, he said unto her, Woman, where are those thine accusers? hath no man condemned thee? She said, No man, Lord. And Jesus said unto her, Neither do I condemn thee:

go, and sin no more. Then spake Jesus again unto them, saying, I am the light of the world: he that followeth me shall not walk in darkness, but shall have the light of life.

John 8:10-12

Jesus was in the temple that day, preaching and teaching the people. The Pharisees and the Sadducees – *the religious people* – went out and took this woman out of bed. It says she was *caught in the very act*. That means that it wasn't *after* the act. It wasn't *thinking* about the act. It wasn't *before* the act. She was literally ripped out of the arms of her lover. We don't know if they dressed her. They seemed to be in quite a hurry to murder her. We don't know what they did with the man or whether they just told him, "Go ahead, get dressed, and follow us because we're going to kill this woman." It takes two to tango, but they didn't mention stoning the man.

> *She was literally ripped out of the arms of her lover.*

They took this woman, *caught in the very act of adultery,* and flung her down before Christ. Jesus, of course, was in the middle of teaching the people. They interrupted Him and indignantly pointed to their object of contempt. "What should we do with *her*?" they demanded. "The law of Moses said we should stone her until she's dead." Silence. The Lord didn't react. Instead, He stopped what He was doing, stooped down, and wrote with

His finger in the dirt. He just moved dirt around with his finger. Irritated with His silence, they continued badgering Him. "What are we going to do with *this woman*?" Jesus was unmoved by their public tirade.

Anytime you feel pressure to react, don't! Pressure doesn't come from the Holy Ghost.

Finally, the Lord looked up at the angry mob. Taking a long deep breath, He addressed her accusers: "Whichever one of you has not sinned, *you* cast the first stone." Then He looked back down at the ground and allowed the Holy Spirit to work. One by one they dropped their stones, their self-righteous fury dampened. Under conviction, they walked away until the only ones left were the woman and this beautiful Rabbi. The people didn't even know *who* this Rabbi was! They just knew that He was a teacher come from God. They didn't know He was the Savior of the entire world.

> *Pressure to react doesn't come from the Holy Ghost.*

The woman was left alone trembling on the ground. Who knows what she looked like! I'm sure she was terrified. Was she roughed up? Did they slap her around? Maybe they had violated her? Perhaps she was half naked? There she was before Christ, the Son of God Himself. Jesus did not look up and say, "Woman, grab some clothes, and get it together."

He looked at her and asked a seemingly obvious question. It was the compassion of God. "Where are your accusers?" For the first time, she looked up from the ground. "Has no man condemned you?" The woman, in her moment of salvation, beheld her Lord. Grasping for comprehension, the unconditional love of Christ washed over her. Indeed, she had no accusers, *not one.* The woman replied, "No man, *Lord.*" As undeserving as she felt, the love of God received her, and she recognized Him as her Lord. She had found her Messiah. How did she know Him? She recognized him by the way He received her. He said to her, "Neither do I condemn thee. Go and sin no more."

> *The woman, in her moment of salvation, beheld her Lord.*

Embraced by Love Himself

Christ laid His life on the line for that woman. In those days it was against the law for a woman to address a Rabbi. Remember the woman with the issue of blood? Do you know that when she came out of her house they could have stoned her? Every single time you see Christ, you see women approaching Him. Think about the woman that washed His feet with her tears and dried His feet with her hair. The men in the room said, "What kind of a woman is this?" Every time you see Jesus, you see women approaching Him, recognizing His *unconditional love* and His *non-condemning* manner. He embraced them with a love and an acceptance that they could not resist.

> *Love embraced her. God is love.*

Think about it for a moment. *Love embraced her.* God is love. She was delivered right in the midst of a murdering mob. When the love of God came into her heart, *she recognized her protector*. He said, "Go, and sin no more." How is that possible, if she didn't recognize Him as Lord? A person can only go and sin no more if they have the power of God. It is the power of God that keeps a person free from sin. Can you imagine? Not only did He save her life, but He saved her soul!

Women of God

Church history identifies this woman as Mary Magdalene. That's tradition. We don't have any scriptural proof that it was Mary Magdalene, but history identifies her as such. Jesus cast *seven devils* out of Mary Magdalene, one of them probably being the devil of lust. After her deliverance, Mary Magdalene hung out with Mary, the mother of Jesus.

Who was Mary, the mother of Jesus? We know that she was a young girl. She was a teenager. But what kind of a woman would God Almighty choose to give birth to the Son of the Living God? Out of all the women on the planet, God chose her! She must have been one courageous woman! Did you know that she became impregnated by the Holy Spirit *before marriage*? In those days, if you were pregnant before marriage, *they would stone you.*

> Mary Magdalene hung out with Mary, the mother of Jesus.

I find it interesting that Mary Magdalene and Mary the mother of Christ had something in common. They were both at risk of being murdered by the religious crowd. Scripture tells us that Mary was the most blessed woman in the world. She was a pure virgin, but where you find Mary the mother of Jesus, you normally find Mary Magdalene. Isn't that remarkable? God is not a respecter of persons! If you lined up Mary, the virgin mother, right next to Mary Magdalene, Jesus would see them both as *totally clean* – absolutely pure in His sight. They were both cleansed by His precious blood. The blood of Christ will remove the spots and blemishes off of *anyone*. He is good to *all* who call on His name. The Lord is not a respecter of persons. All humans need salvation. All humans can be made pure.

> *The blood of Christ will remove the spots and blemishes off of anyone.*

The Spirit of Lust

Mary Magdalene had seven devils cast out of her. It's very likely that one of those devils was a spirit of lust.

A spirit of lust comes on women for different reasons, but normally it's because they've been violated. It comes on them at a young age. When a woman has a spirit of lust on her, she can walk into a room, and the men in the room who are attracted to that spirit will jerk their heads off their necks noticing her. She doesn't even have to be gorgeous. Everyone who is under the influence of that spirit will be attracted to her. Women with a spirit of lust are driven from one relationship to another and never satisfied.

> *A door was opened at one time in their life.*

Why?

A door was opened at one time in their life, and it created a wedge there. That spirit goes in and out, stealing, devouring and ravaging that beautiful woman, time after time. She needs deliverance from the spirit of lust. She may not be possessed, but she can be tormented by that insatiable devil. It's a spirit that follows her and causes her untold heartache and anguish.

Loved into Freedom

The Holy Spirit is welcoming you with arms that are open wide. *Come just as you are.* His grace and His mercy will cover you. Jesus won't condemn you. *He'll love you into freedom.* He'll love you the way you've *never* been loved before! He'll fill that void that's on the inside of you, and you'll never go looking for love in the wrong places again.

*Jesus is not concerned
that you're going to get Him dirty.
He'll take you with seven devils and cast them
out of you. You can wash His feet with your
tears and dry them with your hair.*

Chapter 6

Free from Shame

For with the heart man *(or woman)* believeth unto righteousness; and with the mouth confession is made unto salvation.

Romans 10:10

Righteousness is not a dress or a haircut. Righteousness is something that we *believe unto*. Righteousness is the by-product of receiving Christ into your heart. When a person receives Jesus, the Lord brings *His righteousness* into their life. Justice was satisfied with the blood of Jesus Christ. If God gave His son for humankind, there is nothing He wouldn't do for you!

You don't have anything to prove to anybody. The Bible says you are the righteousness of God in Christ Jesus. It's a free gift. How do you receive the free gift? You believe it, and then you confess it – just like the woman who was caught in adultery. Lift up your hands and say, "I'm righteous, thank God!"

> *There's absolutely no shame in God!*

There's absolutely *no shame* in God! Do you know that Jesus absolutely adores women? Throughout the Bible, people tried to keep women away from Jesus. Remember the woman with the alabaster box? Everybody got mad at her. All she did was worship the Lord with the equivalent of a year's income. She heard God! The Holy Spirit spoke to her. The Lord needed to be anointed for His burial. She walked in where her gift wasn't welcome.

Jesus is your protector. Hallelujah! You do not have to qualify to meet Him. He is not concerned that you're going to get Him dirty. He'll take you with seven devils and cast them out of you. You can wash His feet with your tears and dry them with your hair. He is your example. He is your role model. He doesn't despise a woman because of her upbringing or her past.

He won't turn a woman away because of the baggage that she's carrying. He never stops working on you! You may not get it right the very first time, but you can come back to Him. There is no shame.

> ***For there is no difference*** **between the Jew and the Greek: for the same Lord over all is rich unto all that call upon him.**
>
> Romans 10:12

"There is no difference." Talk about equality! Jesus gave women equal time. He didn't say, "Hush up sister, and be off with you!" He didn't favor one person above another. Mary Magdalene was at the cross when Jesus gave His life for mankind. Standing right next to her was His mother. There they were, side by side.

You're arrayed with the dignity of God.

If you recall, Mary Magdalene had seven devils cast out of her, but apparently she was clean before God! It was also Mary Magdalene who wrapped the body of our Lord in burial cloths. This is recorded in the Word of God for a reason! She handled the body of Christ. Mary Magdalene, out of all people, was chosen by God to be one of the first people to see Jesus after He rose from the dead.

You need not be ashamed! The Lord is rich to all who call

upon Him. You are valuable. You are important. You are clean. You are arrayed with the dignity of God!

Created for Love

What is love? Jesus is love. God is love. Jesus loves women. Before God, there is no difference between male or female. All are lovable in His sight. He is rich to all who call upon His name.

> **For there is no difference between the Jew and the Greek *(and woman) for* the same Lord over all is rich unto *all* that call upon him. For *whosoever (which includes you!)* shall call upon the name of the Lord shall be saved.**
>
> Romans 10:12-13

Jesus is a receiver of women! Did you know that His mother, Mary Magdalene, Joanna and Susanna followed Him around? Joanna, and Susanna gave financially into His ministry. They followed Him, and they served Him. He let them *touch* Him. If God wanted to condemn a person, would He allow that person to touch the very living body of God on earth? You are *not* dirty! You are *not* worthless! In the beginning, God created them male *and* female! God *loves* His creation! You are lovable! You are valuable before God!

Thank God that when I got saved I didn't have a religious upbringing. I didn't know enough to feel condemned! All I knew was that when I met Christ, He said to me, "Where are you accusers? I'm your protector, and no man condemns you." I replied, "No man, Lord." And He said, "Go, and sin no more." That's exactly what I did! I went and sinned no more. It wasn't because someone preached hell, fire and brimstone from the pulpit! I wasn't condemned for the way I looked and acted. I went and sinned no more because I met love. I touched Him! Oh, I met love Himself!

Don't be ashamed because you're beautiful.

In Christ's family there can be no division into Jew and non-Jew, slave and free, *male and female*. Among us you are *all equal*. That is, we are all in a common relationship with Jesus Christ.

Galatians 3:28 The Message

Woman of God, rise up! Grab your gift, and don't hide! God loves you! Don't be ashamed because you're beautiful. That's okay! Don't be ashamed because you're passionate! Jesus loves that. You don't have to apologize for yourself ever again. Yes, submit to one another in love. Respect and honor every human being that God has made, whether they are male *or* female. It doesn't matter. The creation of God is worthy to be honored. Don't sit back in a closet of shame and insecurity because you don't look like a Vogue model!

What is beautiful? You are beautiful. Right now, wherever you are, *you are beautiful*.

Healing in Gilead

Christ is concerned about His women. Anybody that tells you differently needs to have their head examined!

For the hurt of the daughter of my people am I hurt; I am black; astonishment hath taken hold on me. Is there no balm in Gilead; is there no physician there? Why then is not the health of the daughter of my people recovered?

Jeremiah 8:21-22

Jesus is the Word of God made manifest. Jesus is the Word. Jesus is saying, "For the hurt of the daughters I am hurt…"

God is now restoring the health of the daughters of the world. Allow the balm of Gilead to heal you. Allow Him to heal you so that He can use you.

Statistics report that a woman is raped every two minutes. On any given day you can read about the violence that is done to women all over the world: female mutilation, child sex trafficking, molestation, sexual abuse, and sexual exploitation of every kind.

You may say, "I don't want to talk about this. I don't need this." If you don't have a vision, *take mine!* Now is the time to take a stand against violence. Now is the time to hold hands together and pray for the daughters that are being violated in the world. Now is the time for the daughters of God to rise up and receive the healing balm of Gilead. It's not for the psychologists to do! Why are the daughters of this world without help right now? It's because the daughters in the Church are not recovering!

I know, people have pushed you down. People have probably held you back. It may not even be by people around you! It may simply be a general spiritual oppression sent to distract you from becoming everything that God wants you to be.

> *Your faith is always ahead of your experience.*

Now is the time to be healed. There are some things that are settled in heaven, but there are other things that you have to settle in your heart. Settle it, and then go up to God's Spirit-level. Push past oppression into breakthrough. Like the woman with the issue of blood, press into your healing. Press into promotion. Your faith is always ahead of your experience.

The Daughters of God

Daughter, *there is* a balm in Gilead! It's not a temporary fix! When Jesus fixes you, *you are fixed!* It's time for the world to turn its eyes to the daughters of God. The world needs to see the Church healed. You have access to it! When the daughters of God rise up, they will have the answer!

> *You don't have to go through therapy for twenty-five years to be healed!*

The daughters of the world won't have to turn to a secular psychologist to be healed from abuse and multiple personalities. It will be a woman who is filled with the power of God that will say, "I know a God who loves you *just the way you are*. Right now, He will receive you. You don't have to go through therapy for twenty-five years to be healed." Someone has to stand up in the Church and talk about these issues so that the daughters of God can receive their healing. As you step into your healing, the glory of God will shine through you, and the world will turn toward you and say, "How did you do it? Give us the answer!"

Go up into Gilead, and take balm, O virgin, the daughter of Egypt: in vain shalt thou use many medicines; for thou shalt not be cured.

> Jeremiah 46:11

The daughter of Egypt represents the daughters of the world. In vain the world looks for a cure. They are calling the psychic hot lines, they are watching the talk shows, and they're reading the self-help books. They are searching for healing in all the wrong places. Hundreds of years ago, a prophet wrote that the daughters of the world will search in vain. They will try many medicines, but they will not be cured.

Forgiveness

I have prayed with so many women that say to me, "I can't forgive. I hate this person." I tell them I understand.

A person may walk around confessing, "I forgive them, I forgive them." However, in their heart of hearts, *they actually hate them*. The Holy Spirit is a discerner of the thoughts, the intents, and the purposes of the heart. You are naked and opened before Him. All things are known. There is nothing hidden. You are intimately known by your Creator.

> *You are intimately known by your Creator.*

Sometimes the Lord will just say something that will smack you right between the eyes! I can only speak from my personal experience, but I remember being in a service one night after I was saved. In an instant He told me, "You hate this person who abused you." I was sick to my stomach because I had said, "I forgive him." God, in a moment, just took the sword of the Spirit and went *"whoosh!"* He revealed something to me that I was ready to handle.

The Lord will only ask you to do what you're ready to do. He won't take you any further than you're ready to go. If something is too much for you to handle, the Lord won't even reveal it. The only person who can do that for you is the Word of God. Counseling can't do that, but God can.

God is love, and love Himself resides on the inside of you. Love has taken residence within your being. That love will cover a multitude of sins. Yield to love like you would yield to the Holy Ghost. Allow His ability to work in you and to do what you could not do yourself. It's not about feelings. It's not about trying. It's a decision to let go. It's about surrendering to His divine ability. Allow God to love through you. In the process, that love will create a riverbed of provision and blessing in your life.

Love will create a riverbed of provision and blessing in your life.

It's That Easy

How fast did you receive salvation? Was it instantaneous? Somebody is saying in their heart, "Listen, it can't be that easy. I mean, I've gotta walk through this thing." It may be heavy *to you*, but it's not heavy to Jesus. In a moment Jesus told the woman caught in adultery, "Just go and sin no more." Salvation was as simple as believing and confessing. What if you didn't believe it? Could you get saved? No, you couldn't. Why should you complicate an issue that Jesus took care of in one sentence. "Where are your accusers?"

> *It may be heavy to you, but it's not heavy to Jesus.*

There is no distance in the realm of the Spirit. Sometimes the Lord shows me your faces. I *know* you were supernaturally positioned by the Holy Ghost to read this book. God wants to heal your spirit. I want you to put your hands on your spirit and say this:

"Lord, I need Your healing. I need the balm of Gilead to cover my heart. Search my heart. Cover me. Lord, supernaturally heal every wounded area of my spirit. Sweep over me, embrace me with Your love. Reveal to me whatever area I'm ready to be free from. Reveal what I'm ready to see and who I'm ready

to forgive. Father, right now I forgive myself. I release myself from the past. I bind condemnation and torment in my life. Now, Lord, take me to the next level of liberty by Your Spirit. Pour the balm of Gilead on my heart and on my memories. Let Your power consume my being."

> **But for you who fear my name, the Sun of Righteousness will rise with healing in his wings. And you will go free, leaping with joy like calves let out to pasture.**
>
> Malachi 4:2 NLT

You shouldn't have to go to a glamour magazine to receive counseling on your sex life! Jesus is the one who invented sex!

Chapter 7

Self-Preservation

As a young child, I was molested and violently abused by someone that I loved very dearly. This went on from the time I was about three until I ran away at thirteen. I never told anybody what was being done to me. Children have the tendency to take responsibility for things that they are not responsible for. At six years old

I remember thinking, "If I tell someone, there's going to be a divorce in my family." Six years old! How in the world can a child take responsibility for something so heavy? Children are supposed to be protected. Children are supposed to be covered – to be tenderly guarded. A child should never have to deal with the toxic concoction of sexuality, lust, and violence.

At a very young age, I was opened up sexually. The world wonders why their kids are having sex at such an early age. A lot of them have been abused! They're opened up sexually. They're not supposed to feel those feelings. They're not supposed to be open to those feelings. Children are children. They should be filled with healthy emotions. They should know *who their protector is.*

> *At a very young age, I was opened up sexually.*

An innocent child who is bombarded with violence will take *one of two roads*. Statistics indicate that eighty-seven percent of female convicts were violently abused before the age of eighteen. One road leads to prison. The other road produces highly-productive over-achievers. They hold political offices. They run corporations. They have power and influence. These are women who have tremendous clout within the world. I could name names. Women who choose the latter road become control freaks. They don't want anyone to touch them. They build fortresses. They create their own world, their own empires, where they are safe and in control. They were damaged when they lost their innocence, so throughout adulthood, they fashion themselves into a person who is untouchable.

Sparkling Clean

I had a friend who wrote the song "Looking for Love in All the Wrong Places." That's what I did! I looked for love in all the wrong places. I had so many partners that I can't even count them. What does that do to you? What kind of person does that make you? Well, it definitely makes you a sinner! I was a sinner before I did all that. Without Christ, we're all sinners.

> *Maybe you weren't sexually violated, but are you whole?*

My case may be an extreme case. However, I have traveled all over the world and I have asked women about their past. I have asked thousands of women. I can honestly say that one out of every three women has experienced some type of violent abuse.

Sometimes when I address really intimate things, I come up against a wall. I hear people thinking, "Well, you're not talking to me because I was raised in church." Maybe you weren't sexually violated, but are you *whole*? Is there a healing that needs to take place in your life? Is there a wound that has caused you to draw back on life?

Maybe grandpa was a bigot. Maybe grandma was a grandpa beater. Maybe your big brother told you that you were fat so you've over-eaten your whole life. God might show you that! Perhaps you never felt you were worthy of a miracle because you felt unclean.

Perhaps you never felt you were worthy of a miracle because you felt unclean.

God will heal you. The Word of God will wash you. I've got the scrub brush and the Comet! We're going to open you up with the Word of God and rub-a-dub-dub your insides until you're sparkling clean. Then you will shine like a beacon of light. The glory of God will radiate out of your pores. People will run to you because the love of Jesus is flowing out of you like a river.

Jesus Invented Sex

Some women aren't free sexually. Why? They don't know love without shame. It's time to be free from shame. You know, you should be able to run around your house naked, screaming, and shouting, "Honey, come on! Let's go! Wooo!"

You shouldn't have to go to a glamour magazine to receive counseling on your sex life! The counsel you need is here! Jesus is the one who invented sex! *In the beginning,* God made Adam and Eve *and they were naked*! They didn't know. Oh, to be naked and not know! Oh, to be without shame with your husband! God does not want you to have behavior patterns that are hooked into some love affair that you had in the backseat of an automobile.

> Jesus is the one who invented sex!

One of the biggest counseling issues is dealing with married couples who had relations before they got married. They got married, but they brought the ways of the world into that marriage bed. What do I mean? They have flashbacks. They see images. They have thoughts. Those images and thoughts are intruders from the past. They are leftovers from relationships that haven't been *cut off* in the realm of the Spirit. It's a soulish attachment.

Whoever you have *sexual relations* with, you become *one body* with. It's that simple. Leftovers should not be brought into the marriage bed! They need to be cut off forever.

*The moment that you made Jesus Lord,
there was a line drawn in the Spirit.
From that point – all the way back – everything
that's ever happened to your life
is covered by the blood of Jesus.*

Chapter 8

Leave My Women Alone!

Jesus spent His time telling people to leave women alone. "Leave them alone! Let them cry on My feet. Let them dry My feet with their hair. Let them pour anointing oil on Me. Leave the women alone!" We need billboards that declare, "LEAVE THE WOMEN ALONE!"

> The religion scholars and Pharisees led in a woman who had been caught in an act of adultery. They stood her in plain sight of

> everyone and said, "Teacher, this woman was caught red-handed in the act of adultery. Moses, in the Law, gives orders to stone such persons. What do you say?"

John 8:3-5 The Message

The Pharisees brought this woman to Jesus. *Did you know that you can bring anything to Jesus?* You can bring it all to Jesus. By the end of this book, I will teach you how to leave the baggage behind. Jesus wants it. He wants you to give Him the moment you lost your innocence. You can leave it and forget that it ever existed. You can have a supernatural encounter with the Holy Spirit and be set free.

> This they said, tempting him, that they might have to accuse him. But Jesus stooped down, and with his finger wrote on the ground, *as though he heard them not.*

John 8:6

What do you think He wrote? I think He wrote, "I wish these guys would leave My women alone." Maybe He wrote, "Where's the guy?" Now Jesus acted like He didn't hear them. Here's this woman, she's wrapped in a sheet, she just got ripped out of a bed and she's been thrown in the middle of a crowd.

She's a public spectacle. She's trembling in fear and covered in shame. How does the Lord respond? He just bends down and pretends that He doesn't even hear her accusers.

Love Covers

> **So when they continued asking him, he lifted up himself, and said unto them, *he that is without sin* among you, let him first cast a stone at her. And again he stooped down, and wrote on the ground.**
>
> John 8:7-8

Thank God for an anointed statement! He said those words and then looked away. He didn't even get up and try to protect her! You know what protected her? *His words*. His words covered her. I am going to teach you words that will cover you.

Jesus loves women. He loves you! He loves *everything* about you. He loves your hair. He loves your eyebrows. He loves your facials. He loves your lipstick. He loves everything about you! He loves your creativity, your outgoing personality, and your boldness. He loves women. Jesus loves women!

Women are passionate and expressive. Women come into the Kingdom of God and throw up their arms in abandon exclaiming,

"JESUS! OH GOD!!" Women funnel all that passion right towards heaven! Men come into the Kingdom, and they don't even want to lift their hands. They look around to see who is watching. They were trained that way since childhood. Women are passionate creations! Women are expressive! Women were groomed to be passionate!

> **And they which heard it, being convicted by their own conscience, went out one by one, beginning at the eldest, even unto the last: and *Jesus was left alone, and the woman standing in the midst.***
>
> John 8:9

Women funnel all their passion towards heaven!

They all departed, and Jesus lifted Himself up and saw no one but the woman. She was left alone with the Lord.

Grasp this with your heart! *Jesus sees no one but you.* Be transparent with Him. He is so close to you. You are on the inside of Him, and He is on the inside of you. You are intimately connected. There is no room for insecurity. There is no room for pain. You are lovable. You are passionate. Right now, the Holy Spirit has His magnifying glass on your heart. Whatever you're willing to let go of, God will take. Jesus will cover you with His love. He'll do it right now.

Covered by the Blood

When Jesus had lifted up himself, and saw none but the woman, he said unto her, *Woman, where are those thine accusers? Hath no man condemned thee?* **She said, No man, Lord. And Jesus said unto her,** *Neither do I* **condemn thee: go, and sin no more.**

John 8:10-11

Jesus turned toward the woman and said, "Woman, where are your accusers? Has no man condemned you?" I want to ask you that same question. *Where are your accusers?* What's holding you back? When did "can't" enter your vocabulary? "I *can't* do that." Where did that word come from? "I'm *not* cut out for that. I could *never* be like that." Where did all that come from?

Woman, where are your accusers?

The woman replied to Jesus, "No man, Lord." This woman received salvation because she found Jesus, her protector. God

Almighty, who sits in the heavens, did not condemn this woman caught in the very act of adultery. At that moment she had a change of heart and made Jesus her Lord.

No one has the right to condemn you for anything! The moment that you made Jesus Lord, there was a line drawn in the Spirit. From that point – all the way back – everything that's ever happened to your life is covered by the blood of Jesus. Condemnation is *not* your burden to carry. You are a free woman in Jesus. Jesus loves you. If Jesus loved this woman, naked with a sheet wrapped around her, how much more will He love you? You don't have to work your way to His love! You don't have to be the best! You don't have to be the brightest! You don't have to be the prettiest! You just have to know that He is *your Lord*. From that point forward, everything will change!

You don't have to work your way to His love!

Have you been trying to work your way into God's love? Forget it! Maybe it takes somebody like me to make this a reality in your life. I didn't deserve the love of an Almighty God. I didn't deserve that unconditional protection. Maybe it takes a woman like me to say, "Look, you know, I'm like Mary Magdalene. I had seven devils, maybe more, cast out of me." Maybe there are smaller things in your life. Perhaps you haven't had seven devils cast out of you. I think I had more than that cast out of me. I tell people that my husband learned deliverance after he married me!

This is about you in the shower, naked. This is about you in your bathing suit after a long winter. This is about you under the florescent lights in all your glory. The angels don't hide their eyes when you take a shower.

Chapter 9

Secrets to a Great Marriage

Therefore shall a man *leave* his father and his mother, and shall *cleave* unto his wife: and *they shall be one flesh*.

Genesis 2:24

A man must *leave* his father and his mother. Then he is supposed to *cleave* to his wife. "And they shall be one flesh." Do you want to know the secret to a great relationship? There needs to be *a lot of leaving and a lot of cleaving*. That's the secret. **Leave and cleave.**

And they were both naked, the man and his wife, and were not ashamed.

Genesis 2:25

No shame! God paid the price for you to be clean and unashamed before Him. God can see all of you and He loves every part! Somebody is thinking, "What are you talking about?" This is about *you* in the shower, *naked*. This is about *you* in your bathing suit after a long winter. This is about *you* under the florescent lights in all your glory. The angels don't hide their eyes when you take a shower. The glory of God is upon you – naked, full of God, and not ashamed.

Spirit-Mates

After marriage, your husband will be with you, naked and opened in the inner sanctuary. Between the two of you, there will be a three fold union: spirit, soul and body. Not just a body union, and not just a soul union. Women need spirit, soul, *and* body. Women need all three. That's how you were created. You won't be happy without all three.

> *In the world they talk about soul-mates. They just stole the terminology!*

In the world they talk about soul-mates. They just stole the terminology! In the Church there are spirit-mates. Can you imagine being able to communicate with another human being on three levels? You and your husband *united* – spirit, soul, and body.

> **What? know ye not that *your body is the temple of the Holy Ghost* which is in you, which ye have of God, and ye are not your own?**
>
> 1 Corinthians 6:19

Young women, don't fool yourselves! You may be impressed

with those stomach muscles now, but they are going to change! What are you going to do when he gets "Dunlap Disease," and his belly laps over? Those stomach muscles aren't enough to get you through eternity. The "va-va-vooms" are not going to keep you when you're seventy years old, but a spirit connection will!

> *Stomach muscles aren't enough to get you through eternity.*

Have you ever seen a couple at a restaurant, both with newspapers in front of their faces? They're not talking. Why? They don't sharpen each other. There's nothing there.

Iron should sharpen iron. Your mate should be your best friend. Your mate should be your encourager. Your mate should be your covering – somebody who will lift you up. That man should bring out the gifts that you have on the inside of you.

The Strongest Spiritual Weapon

When you beautiful, married ladies go to have relations with your husband, angels are there. So is Jesus. Where would He go? "Oh! Excuse me you guys. I see that you are going to have relations – I'll go wait outside."

He's there! Jesus must think sex is okay! He must think it's cool! He must like the fact that He's in you, and you're in Him. He owns you, and He owns that beautiful man. That union is one of your strongest spiritual warfare weapons against the power of the devil! One will put a thousand to flight, but *two* will put ten thousand to flight.

A woman cannot have relations with a man if she's mad at him. She can't. Resentful? Forget it! Oh yes, you can fake it. If you fake it over a number of years, you're going to be one miserable lady.

> *Jesus must think sex is okay! He must think it's cool!*

What happens if a husband and a wife come together, and the woman all of a sudden bursts into tears? She doesn't have any reason to be crying! Why does that happen? A husband and a wife who join spirit, soul, and body are participating in *God's most powerful weapon within the marriage covenant.* In the midst of it, God will break things off. A supernatural deliverance will take place right within the marriage bed!

> *Sex within the marriage covenant is the most powerful force against the devil.*

Sex within the marriage covenant is the most powerful force against the devil that God ever invented. God invented *one flesh*. God invented sex. That's why the devil does everything he can to get people hooked up to multiple partners.

Soul Ties

What? know ye not that he which is joined to an harlot is one body? for two, saith he, shall be one flesh.

1 Corinthians 6:16

When two human beings are joined in a sexual act there is a link between them. Those two individuals become one flesh. If this happens outside of the covenant of marriage, a soul tie is formed. Soul ties open the door for continued promiscuous relationships, self-esteem issues and repeated victimization.

Those areas have got to be revealed by the sword of the Spirit. God will only reveal to you what you can handle. If something happened to you when you were a little girl, God will just sweep across you with His Spirit. Your eyes will pop open, and you'll see it. You'll know what opened that door in your life. The devil has been getting in through that open door. You have the power to close it right now. The sword of the Spirit will slice that thing. Once you see it, it's revealed. Once it has been revealed to you, it's a done deal.

Flee fornication. Every sin that a man doeth is without the body; but he that committeth fornication sinneth against his own body.

1 Corinthians 6:18

This is not condemnation. This isn't about the past. If you're presently involved in fornication, God will set you free. How do you know you have a soul tie? You know there is a soul tie when you can't stop thinking about the guy. He calls on the phone; but you know you shouldn't be with him. The moment the phone rings, something on the inside of you wrenches. You know it's him before you even pick up the phone! Waves of nausea wash over you and physical symptoms hit your body every time you contemplate ending the relationship. There's no way out.

Soul ties open the door for sickness to lodge itself in a body.

Soul ties open the door for sickness to lodge itself in a body. Women say to me, "I didn't think I was worthy to be healed." They had a memory, and it brought condemnation. God doesn't look at that! God just wants you to be free!

The same power that saved you will heal your physical body. Don't try and understand it with your head. *You didn't get saved in your head, did you?* That same power will heal all the cells in your body and take out the sickness. Let it go. Let Him come in. Don't try to understand it. It doesn't make sense when you go into a hospital for surgery either! They put you under an anesthetic, open you up, and then put you back together again. They tell you that you're healed, and you don't know what they did! *Give Jesus that same opportunity.* Just let Jesus do it. You won't have to get the stitches. You won't have the pain. You won't have to go through chemotherapy.

> *The same power that saved you will heal your physical body.*

The Truth about Physical Manifestations

A lightning bolt is not going to fly from the heavenlies and set you free. Your own mouth will set you free. You will be delivered by your faith-response to the Word of God. How did you become born again? You believed in your heart and confessed with your mouth, *unto* salvation. Your mouth sealed the deal.

Sometimes, when a person gets born again *they feel different*. Other times, *they just know* they were born again. It works the same for every promise of God. You have to believe it and then receive it into your life. Sometimes people wait for some terrific manifestation or a feeling to tell them they've been set free.

Don't allow the devil to rob you in the emotional realm.

A manifestation is not proof that a supernatural transaction has taken place. The proof is that the Word of God says it's true. That's the proof. You believe it, and then you receive it. If God reveals something to you and you have some sort of spiritual experience, fine. If He doesn't reveal anything to you, cool. It's alright either way. There's nothing wrong with you.

Your deliverance is simple. Don't base freedom on an experience. Don't complicate what God has made simple. Don't allow the devil to rob you in the emotional realm. God has made it very easy for you to be free right now. It's a done deal. Don't wait for a voice to thunder out of the sky or for angels to sing. Allow God to heal you.

Tried By the Light

Purge out therefore the old leaven, that ye may be a new lump, as ye are unleavened. For even Christ our passover is sacrificed for us.

1 Corinthians 5:7

Another way to translate this verse is, "Purge out the old, corrupted, sin-conscious part of you, that you may be a new lump, as you are uncorrupted." You are uncorrupted.

How does that happen?

The Word comes in and divides between soul and spirit. The Spirit of God reveals things to you in the secret place of your heart. A light shines in on you. He reveals it. Once you see it, you have dominion over it. Things are only concealed in darkness. Once the light switch has been flipped on, what was concealed is revealed. It's the hidden things of darkness that hold the power of torment in your life. Only the things in darkness cause you to stumble. Once the glory of God shines in on it, there is immediate freedom from oppression.

Closing the Door

How much more shall the blood of Christ, who through the eternal Spirit offered himself without spot to God, purge your conscience from dead works to serve the living God?

Hebrews 9:14

You are purged from death. You are free from sin. It doesn't have a hold on you anymore. You're not a victim anymore. You're free.

If you believe in your heart, God will supernaturally shut doors today. God will shut the door that the devourer has been using to access your life. You don't have to have a devil cast out of you! *All you need is a revelation.* That's all you need! It's just like when you got born again. You had a revelation. That's it! One minute you were going to hell, and the next minute you were saved. It was instantaneous! How about the baptism of the Holy Ghost? "I'm going to lay my hands on you, and you're going to speak in other tongues as the Spirit gives you utterance." In a moment of abandon, you threw up your hands and spoke in tongues. It's not rocket science. It's Holy Ghost!

It's not difficult.

Why do people want to make it a long, grueling process? "You don't understand what I've been through!" He does! He saw you from the moment you were conceived in your mother's womb! He has been watching you! He has been helping you. He has been sending His angels to bring you to the knowledge of His person so that you could be set free. Child of God, it's time to be free!

Pinpoint the moment in your life when you lost your innocence.

I want you to pinpoint the moment in your life when you lost your innocence, whenever that was. Just think about it. The power of God is going to come on you. It may have been in the backseat of a Buick. Wherever it was, remember it.

Now lift up your hands and say this:

"I believe the Word. Be it unto me according to Your Word. Thank you Lord that I am free!"

Pray in tongues, and let the Holy Ghost seal it in your heart.

The world looks good
when you're on magic mushrooms.
The flowers talk, the roses sing
and you see rainbows in front of your eyes.
Why did I need someone's narrow minded
concept of God? I already had all the answers!

Chapter 10

Beyond Brokenness

Like many little girls, I grew up in a dysfunctional home. As an adult, I lived a dysfunctional life, always searching and never satisfied. Early on in my life I had been physically violated. This pattern eerily repeated itself throughout my adult life.

Now the Lord is that Spirit: and where the Spirit of the Lord is, there is liberty.

2 Corinthians 3:17

Before God could use me effectively, He had to heal me thoroughly. He had to bring His liberty into my life and break the chains that bound me to the past. I am a healed vessel. The glory of God has purged out every hurt and every pattern of darkness. My female spirit is *fully healed* and *free from the past*.

> *Before God could use me effectively, He had to heal me thoroughly.*

Where the Spirit of the Lord is, there is freedom. I am a messenger of that freedom. God wants to use you. He wants His power to flow through you. As you read through the coming chapters, know that God is no respecter of persons. What He did for me, He will do for you. Your miracle is at hand.

When Life Lost Its Color

As a little girl, I remember running through the hills of my grandparents' ranch. The grass was green, the wildflowers were in full bloom, and the wind was in my hair. No one had ever told me about a loving God, *but I just knew He existed*. I remember laying on my back under the sun and looking up into the heavens and saying, "God, just let me grow up to help people feel." I was six or seven years old.

Throughout my young life, I watched so many people shut down. They just stopped living. Their life had lost its vibrancy. They were empty shells, void of color, resigned to mere existence. Each day they were sucked into the unending monotony of their miserable eight-to-five job…twenty-four hours a day, seven days a week – working to live and living to work. The weekends would be their only reprieve. Party on Friday. Party more on Saturday. Hangover on Sunday. Monday morning the melancholic cycle would start again. There didn't seem to be any way out.

> *Throughout my young life, I watched so many people shut down.*

Drugs and alcohol numbed the pain. It was terrible when

ATM cards came out. You could go out at three AM, get money for cocaine, and blow your whole paycheck before you came to your senses – anything to fill the gaping hole, anything to numb the desire to dream dreams.

> *Something inside of a person is always hungering to be alive.*

Something inside of a person is always hungering to be alive, to be vibrant, to be passionate, to be creative – to be touchable. Something inside is crying out for that place. People look for it in all the wrong places. I know. I meditated, I swam with the dolphins, I rubbed crystals, I rubbed Buddha's belly. I did anything. I was trying to find something that would satisfy that place on the inside. Ultimately, I found my niche in the field of creative arts.

Searching for Purpose

There is a performance-high within the creative arts field. Hooking into that creative realm is very similar to the anointing. I went to Hollywood. I thought, "Well, that's it right there." I thought the whole world was a lie, so it made sense to be a professional actor. I would just pretend for a living. At least I could get into movies, where I could be all that I wanted to be. I couldn't find it in the world, so I searched for it on the stage. I went to Hollywood and started dancing on a television series called "Solid Gold."

In Hollywood, I threw myself into the entertainment business. It was creative, and it gave me a high. I had discovered some measure of purpose.

> *I had a spirit guide that appeared to me as Marilyn Monroe.*

While in Hollywood, I was heavily involved with Shirley McClaine in the New Age movement. She was like a spiritual mom to me. I had a spirit guide that appeared to me as Marilyn Monroe. My manager in the entertainment industry had managed Marilyn Monroe when she was alive. Consequently, an entity appearing as Marilyn would actually walk into my Hollywood apartment. It would talk to me and tell me what auditions to go to and what to wear. If I obeyed her, I would get the role. If I refused her, I would suffer the consequences.

> *They would chase me down and tell me that I was going to hell.*

I was searching for God.

The only Christians I ever met were the ones in the grocery stores with the polyester suits. They held the little red Bibles, and they were mean! They were aggressive! They would run up to you and grab you. They knew that I needed salvation because I wore bra-less t-shirts, black leather pants and spiked heels. "Of course, she needs salvation. If she was saved, she'd look just like us!" They would chase me down and tell me that I was going to hell.

I didn't believe in hell and I felt sorry for anyone who was naive enough to buy into that bondage. The hell, fire and brimstone just drove me the other way. I wasn't interested in their powerless, polyester Christianity. Give me something real!

I was hooked into the reality of another realm. *I was enlightened.* I was enlightened by Buddha, I was enlightened by Mohammed, the dolphins enlightened me, crystals enlightened me, cocaine enlightened me, and magic mushrooms did wonders – but the Christian in the polyester suit? Forget it!

The world looks good when you're on magic mushrooms. The flowers talk, the roses sing, and you see rainbows in front of your eyes. Why did I need someone's narrow minded concept of God? I already had all the answers!

Freak Accident

One day I ran smack into something that I couldn't fix. I got hurt in what they call a "freak accident." A one hundred and fifty pound door came down and hit me on the back of the skull. I ended up in Cedar Sinai Hospital in Los Angeles, California with morphine pumping in one arm, Demerol shots every three and a half hours, and Percodan every four hours. I spent weeks in the Intensive Care Unit.

When I woke up, I couldn't use my arms or my legs. I was twenty-eight years old, and I was confined to a wheelchair for the rest of my life. I had twenty-three doctors give up on me. After I was released from the hospital, they sent me to a rehabilitation clinic to teach me how to live in a wheelchair.

I had twenty-three doctors give up on me.

I had danced forty hours a week. I was successful. I was independent. I was not the kind of person that you wanted to put in a wheelchair. *I could make things happen.* I didn't need help from anybody. In an instant, I was face to face with a situation that I could not control.

In rehab I learned how to use my hands again. The motor

ability in my brain was permanently damaged, so I couldn't turn a knob, write my name, or even figure out how to work a coffee pot. My hands simply didn't cooperate. I couldn't feel them. They had to put weights on my ankles so that I could feel my legs. If I over-exerted myself, I would go into a seizure. Seizures were a daily, sometimes hourly occurrence. My whole body would convulse violently, and the doctors would be forced to sedate me. I would be unconscious for twenty-four hours at a time. There was no hope. This went on day after day. Days turned into weeks, and weeks turned into months. There was no reprieve.

> *Pain was my constant companion.*

I had been a recreational drug user all my life. I appreciated the high I experienced. All of a sudden, I was addicted to Morphine, Demerol, Percodan and Valium. It wasn't fun. My body needed the drugs, but the drugs didn't help. Morning, noon and night – *pain was my constant companion.* The doctors couldn't help. There wasn't any combination of drugs that could take the pain away.

When they released me from the hospital, I went home to my apartment. I put my phone machine on and sat in my wheelchair. Where were my dreams now? I could see the Hollywood sign from my window. Mocking me, it was like a signpost of failure. I couldn't take it. After sitting in the wheelchair for six months, I decided I would just take control of the situation. The solution was simple. Overdose on drugs, and *go to sleep forever*. No more seizures. No more drugs. No more being dependent on people. I could handle my life before, and I could handle it now. I would just end it all.

Destiny Calling

On the morning of August 23, 1985, I got a phone call from the bass player in a rock and roll band called The Knack. You may have heard of their hit song, "My Sharona." The bass player called me and said, "I want you to go to church with me tonight." Prior to his call, I had decided that I was going to end my life. It was my day to take control of my destiny. Going to church was not how I wanted to spend the last moments

My heart started pounding on the inside of me.

of my life. Before I could turn the invitation down, I heard my mouth reply, "Yes, I'll go." He said "Great!" and then he hung up. I was shocked! Did that really come out of my mouth? My heart started pounding on the inside of me.

I didn't know what to wear. Even when you don't know God, you know that you're supposed to look holy. Oh yes, I had holy clothing! I had holes *here* and holes *there*, but I didn't have a button up blouse! I didn't own a bra. I don't mean to be graphic, but that was just my lifestyle. I worked out forty hours a week. I didn't need one. Everything stayed where it was supposed to!

I finally found a button up shirt and a decent mini skirt. It was the best I could do. It took me three hours to get ready because I had to transfer from my wheelchair to the chair in the shower. Getting dressed was a big deal. Brushing my teeth was a big deal. Everything is an ordeal when your body doesn't work. To complicate the process, if I pushed myself, my body would have gone into another seizure.

> *Everything is an ordeal when your body doesn't work.*

Coasting through Hollywood

After I finished dressing, the phone rang. It was my bass player friend again. He was calling from one of those police call boxes on the side of the freeway. His car had broken down. He told me, "I can't pick you up. I'm stuck on the side of the freeway. Can you get a friend to take you?" I thought, "Oh God, I'm going to call *one of my friends* and tell them I want to go to church? Forget it. They'll take me out and get me high but they're not going to take me to church!"

> *I crawled out of my wheelchair onto the concrete.*

Then I got this wild thought, "I can drive!" Now I had a little black Porsche. It had a clutch and a lot of other bells and whistles. You had to use *everything* to drive it. In an instant, I had this supernatural knowledge that *I could drive.*

Wheeling out into the parking lot, I took the blanket off of my car. It hadn't been driven in six months. I crawled out of my wheelchair onto the concrete and pulled myself up into the Porsche. Somehow I got the thing backed up and then began coasting down the street. This is in Hollywood. It's busy. There's normally lots of traffic. I coasted right across Gower, across

Sunset Boulevard, and then into the Hollywood Presbyterian Church. Nobody was in those intersections. It was a miracle.

I was being propelled by some unseen force.

After I rolled into the church parking lot, I realized that I forgot my wheelchair! I was so concerned about getting there that I neglected to pull the chair into the car. Walking was difficult, but not impossible. I could scoot around if I held onto things. Everything from my hips up was frozen. It didn't move. My neck didn't move either. It was frozen straight forward. I looked like a little old lady. Nevertheless, I scooted out of my car. It felt like I was being propelled by some unseen force. Something was guiding me. Someone was helping me.

Encounter with God

Some people in the parking lot helped me inside the church. It was theatre seating, and there were about fifty Spirit-filled Presbyterians in attendance. The service had already started and the people were singing. I quickly found a seat. At the front of the church, there was a lady strumming three chords on a guitar.

It wasn't very impressive, but it didn't matter. *I heard thousands of voices*. Multitudes of angels were singing. As their voices filled my ears, power permeated my body. Sweat poured down my face, and from deep inside, I started crying – *sobbing*. Nobody had preached a word. Nothing had happened, but I was having an encounter with God. It didn't make sense to my natural mind.

> *Multitudes of angels were singing.*

My friend arrived late and sat down next to me. Heat was pouring out of my body. "Are you alright?" he asked. I didn't know what was going on. I couldn't explain what I was feeling. As I redirected my attention to the front, the minister stood up before the congregation and said, "Jesus Christ is the only way to God." Instantaneously, something lit up on the inside of me! It was like the light switch had been flipped on! All of a sudden, I realized that I had found what I was looking for. It wasn't a big, beautiful church. The people weren't even dressed cool, but I found something. I found the way to God. I found Truth. That Truth went deep inside of me and began to heal my body.

At the end of the service there was an altar call. Of course, I was the only one there that looked like I needed salvation! Several people helped me step out into the aisle. As I shuffled toward the front, the minister stretched out his hand and said, "You're being healed!" The moment those words came out of his mouth, I flew back in the air about ten feet! I just flew back! He didn't touch me. No catcher. No woman-of-the-cloth. I don't know where that mini-skirt went! This unseen power saturated every cell in my body. I was on the floor screaming and crying at the top of my lungs. This beautiful woman of God knelt down beside me on the floor. Wrapping her arms around me, she said, "It's okay baby. It's just Jesus. That's Jesus."

> *Truth went deep inside of me and began to heal my body.*

After forty-five minutes passed, they helped me to my feet. Every ounce of pain had gone from my body. My arms and my legs worked perfectly. I was completely straight. I had taken about fourteen pain pills that day, but I was totally sober and I was totally saved. It was phenomenal.

Hello, This Is God

I met Jesus and received a physical miracle at the same time. *Wow!* I was healed! I was ecstatic. I could feel my arms and my legs. Everything worked! There was no pain!

I didn't know what to do next. I didn't know anyone in the church, so I just decided to get in the car and go home. Driving my car was exhilarating! *VROOOM!* I used my arms and my legs. No more wheelchair! I was free! I was healed! Bounding up the stairs to my apartment, I unlocked the door and went inside. The moment I crossed the threshold a loud, audible voice spoke to me, "THIS IS GOD. YOU'VE BEEN HEALED."

> *The moment I crossed the threshold, a loud, audible voice spoke to me...*

I stayed in my apartment for two days. The audible voice told me, "I want you to take all your medication and throw it in the dumpster outside. You're going to go through withdrawals for two days, but you're going to be alright." During that time period, the audible voice told me, "I want you to go through your house and throw out all of your occult items, your books, your tarot cards – all the psychic paraphernalia. Put it in a box and throw it away." I did exactly what the voice said because it was the voice of God.

> **My sheep hear My voice, and I know them, and they follow Me.**
>
> John 10:27

For two days I laid on my bathroom floor – vomiting, sweating, and shaking. I went through withdrawals like a heroine addict. I didn't sleep.

During that time, God told me stories from the Old Testament. He told me stories! He told me about Joshua, Moses, and Balaam. I had never heard them in my life. Thirty-six hours later, my whole system was completely cleaned out, just like He said. The fire of God stayed on my body for ten days.

Appointment with Power

The night I got my miracle, there was a young man team-ministering with the man who preached. His name was Christian Harfouche. I returned to the church a week later because I wanted to tell somebody what happened to me. I was so excited! When I went back, I met that young man again and he asked me to go to a Bible Study. That's a Christian date. I didn't know what I was getting myself into!

The Bible Study was held at a house. When I arrived, everyone was holding hands in a circle. Fascinated, I walked toward the group. As I approached, the leader of the Bible study turned around and said, "Today, the Lord told me that you were going to be here and that He is going to fill you with the…" Immediately power surged through my body. I fell to the ground. I didn't understand what was going on. One minute I was standing, fully coherent, and the next I was flat on my back. Strange words were coming out of my mouth. My mind couldn't process the language. I didn't know where it came from! Shocked, I looked up from the floor, and asked, "*WHAT* was *that*?!" "You just spoke in other tongues." the leader replied. Later, they

> *God will always meet you at your point of obedience.*

explained that I had received the baptism of the Holy Spirit. It was unlike anything that I had ever experienced. It was absolutely awesome!

I was afraid to disobey God because I thought if I did I would lose my miracle. Consequently, I did everything God told me to do. *EVERYTHING*. Sometimes I didn't want to but I did it anyway. God will always meet you at your point of obedience.

Now Is Your Time

A healed woman is a powerful woman. A woman that has been released from the scars and battle wounds of the past can be used as an effective conduit of God's power. She can go anywhere and do anything for God.

Right now, you have an appointment like I did. You have an appointment with Jesus. This is *your time*. Maybe you haven't been walking with God. Maybe you've been trying to do things in your own strength. If you're ready to come back to Him, pray this out loud right now:

> *A healed woman is a powerful woman.*

"Lord Jesus, I know You're the only way. I know there's no other way. You are God. Right now, touch me. This is my appointment with destiny. I give my heart to You. I give everything I am to You. I am forever Yours. Fill me with Your power."

Now, I'm going to pray for you. There is no distance in the realm of the Spirit. You don't need me to come to your house and physically lay hands on you. I'm going to release the miracle power of God on your life *through words*.

I want you to place your hand on the part of your body that needs a miracle. With your faith, you are going to *grab every word* that applies to you. Just reach out and grab it. *It's yours*. The power of God is going to come upon you. The creative power of the Holy Spirit is going to overshadow you just like it came upon Mary, the mother of Jesus. I want you to repeat my prayer for you out loud and then receive your miracle. What God did for me, He will do for you.

> *There is no distance in the realm of the Spirit.*

Lord, I ask for the miracle anointing of God. I ask for the power of the Holy Spirit to touch Your daughter. I curse every physical aliment. Touch lungs. Touch bones. Touch herniated discs. Touch arthritis. Heal your daughter in every area right now, Lord. Open ears that haven't been able to hear. Melt cataracts off eyes. Inject blood with life. I bind every form of cancer right now. I bind every form of blood disease. I bind diabetes. I loose the power of God on you from your head all the way down to your feet.

Now check yourself. Move your body. Earlier, I taught you how to receive a miracle. *It's just like salvation.* I received Jesus and my miracle at the same time. God is no respecter of persons. What He did for me, He will do for you.

How do you do it? You believe in your heart, and you confess with your mouth. God wants your hope to take hold of His faith. Faith is never activated until you do it. You hear the Word, and then you step out on the integrity of that Word.

> *Faith is never activated until you do it.*

I want you to begin to move your body in accordance with what you believe just happened. It doesn't matter if you heard angels or if you didn't hear angels. We live by faith, not feelings. We rely on the integrity of the Word of God. Go ahead and continue to move your body until every symptom has left.

*When you begin to move in miracles,
you actually start with headaches and colds.
You start with small things, and as your
faith grows, you work your way up.*

Chapter 11

Astounding Miracles

All miracles are phenomenal. They are all absolutely amazing. However, there is one in particular that I clearly remember. It was one of the first absolutely astounding miracles that I participated in.

During a service, this beautiful mother brought her six month-old child to my husband and me. The child was born with severely deformed legs, and the medical prognosis was dim. The only hope for the child to ever walk was to reset the legs. The following day, the doctors were planning to break the baby's legs and realign them. After the procedure, the baby would be confined to a full body cast until the bones had properly fused. Even then, there was no medical guarantee that this procedure would enable the child to walk. The parents were desperate.

We had ministered in the healing anointing and we were preparing to dismiss the people. The service was over and we were ready to go home. As we turned to leave, this beautiful mother ran up to us. Her baby was wrapped in her arms. Almost pleadingly, she asked us if we would be willing to say a prayer for her little baby. Desperation filled her eyes. I began to weep as the compassion of God welled up from the inside of me. We laid our hands on the child and just said, "In the name of Jesus, heal this beautiful baby." The glory cloud didn't sweep into the room. We didn't sense the rain of the Holy Spirit. There wasn't an immediate manifestation. We just prayed the prayer of faith. The woman thanked us and then turned around and left.

> *The compassion of God welled up from the inside of me.*

The next night the mother came back. She was ecstatic! She stood before the church with her child and testified to what God had done. After going home, she put the baby in the crib. The child was scheduled for corrective surgery the following day. Tucking the baby in, she started to walk out of the room. As she was walking out, she froze in her tracks. Cracking sounds were coming from the direction of the crib! This is a true story! Running back to her child, she looked down and watched as God supernaturally reset the child's legs. In front of her eyes, the legs straightened out and became absolutely perfect. The Holy Ghost performed a surgery in the crib as mom watched! The following day, she brought the baby and showed us. The baby was perfect! It was supernatural! I know it sounds amazing, but it's true!

> *The Holy Ghost performed a surgery in the crib as mom watched!*

Miracle on the Frontier

Alaska, they say, is the last great frontier. It's a majestic land of ancient glaciers, spectacular Northern Lights, and endless miles of tundra. Thousands of Native Alaskans, or Inuit's (Eskimos), call this land home. In the native villages, life is simple, and the people are happy to live off the land.

I have ministered in the remote villages of Alaska several times. The people are beautiful, and they hold a special place in my heart. One village in particular was twenty-eight miles off the coast of Siberia, just off the Bearing Sea. Everything was frozen. Glaciers were all around. On a toasty day, summertime temperatures range from thirty-four degrees to forty-eight degrees. On the day I arrived, it was sixty degrees *below zero* with winds gusting at sixty miles per hour. It was *cold!*

> *On the day I arrived, it was sixty degrees below zero.*

The village was made up of six hundred Native Alaskans who were governed by their tribal elders. The weather was frigid, but the people were warm and friendly. I had brought warm clothes, but nothing had prepared me for this! They bundled me up in a huge seal coat with a fur encased hood. I looked like a real Inuit! We took three small planes to get there, and the last plane had to land on ice. There was no airport. We were picked up by the villagers on snowmobiles, as there were no roads. Everything was white.

We also flew in a cargo plane full of food for the village. Since Native Alaskans subsist off the land, they aren't able to enjoy all the beautiful foods that we have. For the most part, they harpoon whale, walrus, and other marine mammals. They also hunt fox and reindeer. Fresh fruits, oranges and apples are a rare and exotic treat for them. The people were delighted.

They gave me a cold high school auditorium...

I was scheduled to minister for several days in a row. They gave me a cold, high school auditorium and a little karaoke machine. No beautiful music or sophisticated lighting. It was just me and the people, and they were so hungry. The harvest was truly ready. The lost were waiting. After preaching the Gospel, they all got saved. Then I asked for the sick to come forward. Hundreds of them streamed down from the bleachers.

The only church in the village was a Presbyterian church with a pastor from China. They had never experienced the power of God! I began to minister to the people individually in a prayer line. As I laid hands on them, they fell out in every direction! They would giggle, cry, and fall out – just like they knew what they were doing! They loved the power of God. It was beautiful.

As I moved down the line, I came to a mother with a child in her arms. In her gorgeous Inuit accent she pleaded, "*Please! My baby!* She is two years old and has never been able to walk." Looking down at the child in her arms, I noticed that one of her small legs was withered and wrapped up beneath her. When the child moved, all she could do was scoot along the floor. I laid my hands on the baby, and I said, "Mama, take the baby home and bring her back tomorrow. I will show you how Jesus Christ will make this child stand, walk, run and play."

> *Jesus Christ will make this child stand, walk, run and play.*

The next morning she brought the baby to the meeting. As I was going down the prayer line again, I came to the mother. The Holy Ghost reminded me of what I had said to her the previous day. This child was going to be whole! I touched the mom and said, "Mom, is *that* the child I prayed for yesterday?" She nodded. Gesturing towards her little girl, I asked if I could hold her. The mom handed me her baby.

As I held the child in my arms, I instructed her, "Now straighten out your legs." Immediately, the leg straightened out! The withered leg just popped right out! It happened right in my arms! I placed her on the floor, and she stood straight up like she had done it a million times before! Picking her back up into my arms, I said, "Mom, go down to the other end of the gym, bend down and open your arms. This baby is going to *run* and *jump* into your arms." Then I told the little girl, "Now you run to your mother!" Just like that she took off running and jumped into her mama's arms! It was awesome. It was absolutely awesome!

Divine Initiative

There were so many miracles! While we were waiting for a plane to the village, there was an Inuit woman in a wheelchair. The flight attendants were extremely upset because they couldn't get her on the plane. She was fresh out of knee surgery, maybe a day earlier, and was on her way back to the village. She was in *excruciating* pain. Every time the flight attendants tried to move her, she would scream in agony.

> *We were smack-dab in the middle of a God opportunity.*

Now here you are in the middle of a public place – *just like Jesus* was when He walked through the streets of Galilee healing the sick. We were smack-dab in the middle of a God opportunity.

I walked over to the lady. The flight attendants were frantically trying to calm the woman down. I bent down and looked into the woman's eyes. She had the most gorgeous blue eyes and this incredible Native Alaskan face and jet black hair. Looking into her eyes I said, "I'm coming to your village because I heal the sick. I heal the sick in Jesus' name. Is it alright if I just put my hands on you?" Tears welled up in her eyes and began to stream down her face.

Placing my hands on her, I released the love of God into her. She fell out under the power, in the wheelchair! The flight attendants weren't sure what was going on, so they just began to back up. I really didn't care. This woman just needed a miracle.

> *Placing my hands on her, I released the love of God into her.*

The flight attendants called for assistance, and some strong men came and carried her in the chair down the stairs, out into the snow, and then up into the airplane. They sat her down directly behind me. She was out under the power for the whole thing – *the entire time!*

The plane took off. In the middle of the flight, someone tapped me on my shoulder. Turning around, I looked over into the inquisitive eyes of the woman. *She had just woken up.* "I feel funny." she said. Smiling, I asked, "Well, do you have *any* pain?" She said, "No! I feel incredible! I want to go to the ladies room." I said, "Well just get up and go." She said, "Okay." Moving out of her seat, she *walked* to the ladies room!

When we landed, there was snow everywhere, and the stairs coming down from the plane were steep. The flight attendants brought the wheelchair to the front of the plane. When the woman saw the wheelchair, she retorted, "No, I don't need a wheelchair. *God healed me.*" Getting up, she walked straight down the stairs off the plane! Her husband was waiting for her, expecting her to be in a wheelchair. She just walked right down the stairs and wrapped her arms around him. He wrapped his arms around her and they just held each other. Walking by, I thought, "Isn't that just like God?" Hallelujah!

Several nights later, I was preaching in the village church. They told me that the Inuit people always arrive late. I had prayed, and I had fasted. It was cold, and I was there. I had a destiny. I had a mission. I had a purpose. I wasn't playing around.

An hour before the church opened, it was packed out. People were overflowing into the streets, waiting to get in. There was standing room only.

As I was preaching, the woman who had been healed on the plane walked right into the church! It was apparent that she had never been in a church before. Everyone watched as she walked straight down the middle aisle, interrupted me mid-sentence, and wrapped her arms around me! She didn't know she wasn't supposed to do that! Brimming with excitement, she said, "I've been looking for you for two days! I've been going from church to church to find you because I wanted to tell you that I am totally and completely healed!" God is so awesome! As she had her

> *"No, I don't need a wheelchair. God healed me."*

arms around me, the power of God hit her. She started laughing and crying in the Holy Ghost. Then she fell out under the power of God. It was beautiful. When she got up, she said, "Thank you," and walked down the aisle and out of the church!

> *The Lord is so much more interesting than we can imagine.*

The Lord is so much more interesting than we can imagine. If we will follow Him, He will do amazing things!

Dealing with Healing

People say, "Well, how do you do miracles? Is that a special thing that only some people can do?" Jesus said *go ye into all the world.* He said to lay hands on the sick, and they shall recover. He said this to believers. *Every believer* can lay hands on the sick and see them recover.

In the beginning of the 90's, my husband and I decided to get aggressive with sickness and disease. It was our enemy, and we wanted to go after it. We began to aggressively attack it in every form.

> *Every believer can lay hands on the sick and see them recover.*

We would pull people out of wheelchairs. My husband would hit people in their stomachs, and tumors would dissolve. I know that sounds wild, but the Holy Ghost would tell him to do it. An unction would come on him, and he would step out in the gift of faith under a supernatural directive.

In normal circumstances, a person would double over in pain if you socked them in the stomach or yanked them out of a wheelchair. However, when the gift of faith is in operation, they just get healed.

It took me awhile to step out in that gift because I didn't want to move in presumption and hurt someone! The first woman that I ever hit in the stomach had a tumor the size of a five month old pregnancy. This gift came on me, and I just went *"POW!"* Her skirt fell off because the tumor instantly dissolved! Thank God it was a women's meeting!

When you begin to move in miracles, you actually start with headaches and colds. You don't just wake up to the ability to pull someone out of a wheelchair! The Lord will start you out with small things, and as your faith grows, you will work up to *seemingly* bigger things. It's a progression. The Lord leads you in that progression so that you don't move in presumption, but by the power of His Spirit.

> *When you begin to move in miracles, you actually start with headaches and colds.*

The Working of Miracles

I remember the first time that we ever pulled somebody out of a wheelchair. We had just finished a miracle service, and we were preparing to leave. It was one of those meetings where everybody in the building got their miracle – e*verybody.* People couldn't even get within twenty feet of us without falling out under the power.

It had been a tremendous meeting, and the people were ready to go home. You could feel it. They had been there for five hours already, and they were tired.

My husband was standing in the pulpit and said, "Well, I guess there is nobody else here that needs a miracle. We'll just wrap up the service and go home." All of a sudden, from the back of the auditorium, this person started yelling, "Wait! Wait! Wait!" We watched as this woman was rolled down the aisle in a wheelchair. She had never used her legs in her life – thirty-three years in that wheelchair! She had thirteen different forms of arthritis, and her knees were bent and appeared glued together. Her feet were turned out at the bottom, so if you stood her up, she would actually be

People couldn't get within twenty feet of us...

standing on her ankles.

We thought, "Oh my, the people want to go home." You could feel the pull of the people. They were exhausted, but this woman had come for her miracle! My husband and I looked at her, and we just said, "Okay." We put our hands on her and *there was no gift of great faith*. Fire did not come down from heaven. *We didn't feel a thing*. We just knew that everybody was tired, and the service was over. It's like a bar at two in the morning when the lights go on. It's over! The service was over.

We laid our hands on her and prayed the prayer of faith. At this point in our ministry, we had never witnessed a *severely* crippled person come out of a wheelchair. There's a progression to your faith.

We put our hands on her and there was no gift of great faith.

I'll never forget it. My husband said to her, "Why don't you do something that you've never been able to do before." She reached out her hands, and grabbed our hands and stood up. When she stood up, she stood on her ankles. Her feet were turned out flat, and her knees were still stuck together. I was pretty much convinced that this woman was *not* healed. I thought, "If this was a miracle, her feet would have flipped back in, her knees would have come apart, and she would have been running!"

God was teaching me that there is a *working of miracles*.

Sometimes you have to actually *work* a miracle. Getting down on my knees, I put my hands on one of her feet and I began to pray. I said, "In the name of Jesus!" All of a sudden, one foot went *"Pop!"* and snapped back into place! Then I put my hands on the other one, and it did the same thing! I watched it! Then her knees disconnected, and she stood straight up. We started walking her around!

She did not want to stop walking! The people were exhausted. They had been there a long time, and they were ready to go home. In the realm of the Spirit I could hear the people saying, "Shut down the meeting!" There was so much pressure from the people. They didn't realize the magnitude of the miracle taking place. They were not in the flow. They just wanted to go home.

> *God was teaching me that there was a working of miracles.*

We were walking with this woman, and she was still very wobbly. Still, it really didn't look like a miracle to me. Yes, her feet had popped in. Yes, her knees had separated. Yes, she was walking. I thought, "If this is a real miracle, she'll let go of our hands, stand straight up and start running."

She had us walking her around for twenty minutes! She would not sit down! Finally we said to her, "You've got to sit down." We had to end the meeting and release the people. With great resolution, she firmly replied, "I have been in this wheelchair for thirty-three years, and *I am not sitting down!*" My husband and I left the meeting. She continued walking around the auditorium.

Naturally Supernatural

My husband and I returned to the hotel. This was in Hollywood. He went to one side of the bed, and I went to the other side of the bed. We were exhausted. We started taking off our clothes and, all of a sudden, we both looked at each other and said, *"OH MY GOODNESS! SHE HADN'T WALKED IN THIRTY-THREE YEARS!"* It was like a light bulb went on! We both started crying.

Later we received the report that she was completely healed and no longer needed a wheelchair.

> *There is no distance in the realm of the Spirit.*

When you're in the realm of the Spirit, it's natural to be supernatural. *It's so natural.* The supernatural feels entirely natural! You see things and know things that you would never be able to ordinarily know. It's natural for a Christian to be supernatural! It's natural for you to see in the Spirit. It's natural for you to feel the healing virtue come out of your hands. It's natural for you to get a word of knowledge and a word of wisdom. It's natural for you to flow in the things of the Spirit. It's natural for you to fall into a trance, go to heaven, and come back again! It's natural! It's totally natural!

Everything Danced

A week after I got my miracle, I rented a dance studio in Hollywood on La Cienega Boulevard. All I had was an Amy Grant tape. I took the tape to the studio, slipped it into the cassette deck, and turned up the volume. The music filled the empty studio. It was just God and me. Looking at my reflection in the long vertical mirrors, I told the Lord, "God, *if I'm healed*, then I will be able to dance *just like I danced before I got hurt.*"

I wanted to know how thorough the job was. I had been in a wheelchair for six months. The doctors told me that I could never dance again. There was no hope. The case was closed, my dancing career was over. Then God instantly healed me. But had my body recovered from *months of inactivity*? Were the dancer's muscles intact? Was I still *the dancer*? I was determined to find out.

> *The music was playing, and it was just God and me.*

I locked the door to the studio. For the time being, it was my "God space." I didn't want anybody to see me. This was personal. This was between God and me. I was there to test the miracle, but I also wanted to worship God with every fiber of my being. Everything in me wanted to dance! There was so much to let out! Dance was my form of expression. This was my opportunity to communicate my worship and adoration before God. I was alone, so I started moving to the music.

One week after I had gotten out of the wheelchair, I did *quadruple pirouettes*. I did triple pirouettes, leaps, and jumps! Oh, I danced and danced and danced! I worshipped God with every part of my being. I used *every* muscle. Everything worked. *Everything danced*. I was *still* the dancer.

> *I was seeing white. All I saw was the glory of God.*

I wasn't looking in the mirrors. My eyes were gone. All I could see was white. The glory of God filled the studio. I was somewhere else, but my body was moving and worshipping Jesus.

All of a sudden, I fell out under the power of God on the hardwood floor. I laid there, panting, crying, and rejoicing. As I was laying on the floor, I heard this voice inside my heart. It was *my* voice. It was me. I said, "Lord, what am I going to do now?"

Have you ever asked a question in the quiet place of your heart? Sometimes I hear myself say, "God, if you don't help me, I can't do this!" I hear these little "Robin things" on the inside.

Then I heard the voice of God answer my silent question. He gently replied, "Up until this point you've been the director of your life. Right now, I'm writing a new script, and I'm going to direct your life." It was beautiful. It was God. Then all of a sudden, as if on cue, this light streamed in through the window. Warm rays of magnificent sunlight shined down on me. I began to praise God for what He had done in my life.

> *Have you ever asked a question in the quiet place of your heart?*

The bedroom disappeared.
All of a sudden
I found myself at the feet of this giant.
There were angels
and chariots flying above Him.

Chapter 12

Visions and Revelations

Several months later, I married that young preacher, Christian Harfouche. One day, while we were laying in bed, the presence of God swept into the room. We were just laying there, and this Holy Spirit mist started filling the room. Thank God my husband knew so much about the Word, because I would have been wiggy without him. I didn't know anything! For years he wouldn't let me read the book of Revelation or the Old Testament. All he would let me read were the Gospels and the Epistles. He didn't want me to get confused.

I was a year old in the Lord, and I had never read the book of Revelation. The cloud of Glory just filled our bedroom. We were relaxing on the bed, and my husband had his hand on my tummy. When the tangible presence of God entered the room, power started surging out of my husband's hand and going into my spirit. It was like water gushing out of a fire hose. It was phenomenal! That out-flow of power immediately thrust me into an open vision.

> *Power started surging out of my husband's hand and going into my spirit.*

Paul the apostle said, "In the body or out of the body, I do not know." There are different kinds of visions. There are mini-visions that you have on the inside where you catch a glimpse of something. It's not exactly like your eyes are closed, and it's not exactly like your eyes are open. You just see something. Then there's the open vision, where you actually see it with your eyes. It's like looking out, and, all of sudden, everything you see in the natural disappears. I was one year old in the Lord and I was translated into this open vision. The bedroom vanished.

Suddenly, I found myself at the feet of this giant. There were angels and chariots flying above Him. He had nail prints in His hands and nail prints in His feet. A sword was coming out of His mouth and His eyes were lit up with fire. He was standing on top of a seven-headed dragon, and there were demons running in terror in every direction.

At the end of the vision, I saw this road that led up to a city in the sky. The road didn't light up until I looked at it. When I looked at it, it lit up before me. The light that was radiating from the road was like nothing I had ever seen. It didn't resemble anything within our present technology. The city was solid gold and brilliant. Light emanated from within it.

I was gone for ten or twelve minutes. When I came back, the glory gradually left the room, and I was able to talk. I told Christian what I had seen, and the Lord instantly downloaded the interpretation into him.

He said that the giant was the Body of Christ. In the last days, the Body of Christ will stand on top of all the power of the devil. The seven-headed dragon represented every face of evil. The eyes of fire stood for the discernment that is going to be in the Body of Christ. They will be able to discern. The Body will be able to see in the realm of the Spirit. Everything will be lit up by the fire of God coming out of their eyes. They'll be able to go in to the realm of the Spirit and know things. Then he said the sword coming out of the giant's mouth represented the Word of God. It's powerful; it's sharper than any two-edged sword. The nail prints in His hands and in His feet testify to our standing in Christ: We are crucified with Christ, yet we live. When people see us, they will see Christ in us.

> *At the end of the vision, I saw this road that led up to a city in the sky.*

> **To them God willed to make known what are the riches of the glory of this mystery among the Gentiles: which is *Christ in you*, the hope of glory.**
>
> Colossians 1:27 NKJV

I came out of that vision and God imparted to us the ability to deal aggressively with sickness and disease. We were given an authority that we had never experienced before. A new *boldness* came on us. It was different from anything that we had ever experienced.

> **Therefore I remind you to stir up the gift of God which is in you through the laying on of my hands.**
>
> 2 Timothy 1:6

Stolen Miracle

The next week I was in a meeting and this gentleman walked up to me. He was a minister of the Gospel and I greatly respected him. Taking me aside, he explained that he had a word from the Lord for me. He said, "You're going be tried just like Peter was, but Jesus wanted me to tell you that you're going to make it."

I didn't understand, but I received the word into my spirit. I went home and within three days I had lost my miracle – flat out. I couldn't walk. I was in pain twenty-four hours a day. I had been healed for one year. Everything was perfect. I was a documented medical miracle. This man spoke this word, and within a matter of days, my body was totally crippled again. I was rushed to the hospital and placed in the intensive care unit. They hooked me up to Morphine and Demerol. Everything hurt.

> *I went home and within three days I had lost my miracle.*

I didn't understand. On the inside of myself I was saying, "What did I do wrong to end up back here? Where did I go wrong? What did I do?" I stopped doing dope, I stopped doing drugs, I married the preacher, I left the entertainment business. I did everything that I ever heard God tell me to do. Where did I miss it?

Words carry power. They can either be full of the power of God or full of the power of the devil. There are words of blessing and then there are words of cursing. *Both carry power.*

There are words of blessing and then there are words of cursing.

That gentleman was a minister of the Gospel, but he tapped into the wrong realm. He then released the power of that realm with his mouth. I was a baby Christian and he was a minister of the Gospel. I didn't know. I didn't understand. The devourer harnessed those words and it hit my spirit like a poisonous dart. Within days, those words had produced fruit and I *"lost"* my miracle.

City in the Sky

I was totally crippled again. They placed me in intensive care and hooked me up to a twenty-four hour Morphine drip. Demerol shots were administered every three and a half hours, Percodan every four hours, and there were pills on top of that to stop the seizures. I was strapped to a bed all over again. The doctors didn't understand. Twenty-three doctors couldn't explain how I got healed in the first place, and they certainly couldn't explain why I was crippled again.

While my husband sat there in the hospital room, an intercessor called. He told Christian, "The Lord spoke to me and told me that the key to Robin's healing is in the open vision that she had several months ago." My husband turned to me and said, "You're going to tell me the vision of the giant." He said, "We're going to write it down. You talk and I'll write." I couldn't hold a pen.

> *I was strapped to a bed all over again.*

Strapped to the hospital bed, I began to retell the vision. As I spoke, the glory cloud came into the room. For forty-five minutes the door to my unit didn't open. Prior to that, nurses had been checking on me every five minutes. There must have been an angel with a flaming sword at the door! No one came in!

The room filled with the presence of God. As I retold the vision about the giant standing on the dragon, everything disappeared. The hospital room, the blinking monitors, the tubes – *everything vanished.*

> **For instance, I know a man who, fourteen years ago, was seized by Christ and swept in ecstasy to the heights of heaven. I really don't know if this took place in the body or out of it; only God knows.**
>
> 2 Corinthians 12:2 The Message

I found myself once again at the bottom of the lighted road. It was lit up before me. I looked up and saw the brilliant city that was in the sky. Jesus Christ was standing in front of the city, and there was an angel on His right and an angel on His left.

The angelic beings had to be nine feet tall! They wore gold armor and white garments beneath. Jesus was in a white garment, and His face looked like the sun. He was the color of bronze. When I looked at him, I was immediately drawn to the holes in His feet.

While I gazed at His feet, He motioned to me to come, and I was instantly at the top of the lighted road. Just like that, I was there! I didn't walk there. I don't know how I got there, but instantly I was right in front of Him.

He wrapped His arms around me and just rocked me. As He held me in His arms, I felt the balm of Gilead come upon my head and run down to my feet. As His love covered me, all the pain left my body through the bottom of my feet. He continued to hold me in His arms and rock me.

> *He wrapped His arms around me and just rocked me.*

The Sound of Heaven

When He released me, He turned toward these big gates and opened His arms. When he did, the gates opened up on their own accord. Jesus took me by the hand and walked me in.

I saw the streets of heaven! They were transparent gold. I saw people walking, but they weren't touching the ground. They were dressed in brilliant clothes. They looked like they were lit up from the inside-out. There were buildings made out of gold and people looking out of the buildings. Everybody saw me, but they looked right through me. No one spoke to me. They knew me, and I knew them.

I saw the streets of heaven! They were transparent gold.

Jesus never let go of my hand. He brought me to this huge temple with giant pillars. I looked down into the temple, and I heard a sound that resembled thunder, like the sound of a tremendous roar. It was the sound of many waters or like a huge waterfall. There were variations and combinations of waterfall sounds and sounds of thunder.

I didn't know where the sound was coming from until I looked down and saw multitudes of people. There were dancers on the floor. With all of their heart, they were dancing and leaping and praising God. There were layers upon layers of people. As high as my eye could see, there were balconies with people. Their arms were lifted up to God in praise and adoration. I felt this lightening bolt of power go through my body, and I said, "Lord, what are you doing?" He said, "I'm tuning you in to the worship of heaven."

> *"I'm tuning you in to the worship of Heaven."*

The Miracle Move of God

All of a sudden, we were somewhere else. We were in this room, and there was a throne there. There was a big lion, but he looked lovable, not fierce. He was magnificent and beautiful.

Jesus said to me, "There's a creative miracle wave that's going to hit the earth before I come back." He showed me this pool filled with body parts: hearts, lungs, legs, spines – *everything*. It wasn't gross or weird. It was just a pool full of every body part imaginable. It was a pool full of creative miracles. While I stared at the pool, He said, "Satan has been able to counterfeit everything that I'm doing, but he can't create. He's not the Creator. I'm the Creator. Before I come back, I'm going to release a miraculous move of God where people all over the earth will see the power of My hand. All over the earth they will be given the opportunity to know that I am God before I come back."

> *"There's a creative miracle wave that's going to hit the earth."*

The Spirit of Pain

Then He said to me, "You know, if you would have rebuked the spirit that affected your body, he would have had to leave you." Shocked, I replied, "But Lord, it wasn't a spirit. I got crippled again!" He said, "No, *that was a spirit of pain*." The Lord went on to explain, "If you would have rebuked him, he would have had to leave." Then I said, "Well, what is the spirit of pain?" He said, "That is *the door opener* for every other disease." I still didn't understand what the Lord meant so He elaborated. He said, "When people get pain, they don't know what it is. It's considered a warning signal for every type of disease. When you have pain and don't know what it is, you go to the doctor. They give you a list of what it could be. Then they start testing you. They want to find out what your father or mother died of or what runs in your family. They go down the list to see if there was blood disease, diabetes, heart symptoms, spinal meningitis, arthritis, or bursitis. Then they begin to put you through a series of tests to find out exactly what you might have. It's called a prognosis."

> *"If you would have rebuked him, he would have had to leave."*

That's why it's called *practicing medicine*. I'm not against doctors, but I know the Healer. I'd rather be healed by Him than cut open and stitched back together!

Then He continued, "When people have pain, they go the doctor and have a series of tests. Then the other spirit comes to enforce *what they believe they have*. Pain opens the door. Anytime you rebuke the spirit of pain, he will have to leave."

Anytime you rebuke the spirit of pain, he will have to leave.

When you're in heaven, you don't want to come back. I wasn't given a choice! The Lord looked into my eyes and said, "I am commissioning you today to go back to the earth." This was 1986. He said, "I want you to be My eyes and My hands."

Instantly I woke up in the hospital room. I ripped the IV's out of my arm, got up out of that bed and told the doctors goodbye. You should have seen their faces!

Vendetta against Darkness

I have a personal vendetta against pain! I have a vendetta against him because he messed with me!

Through the power of the Holy Spirit, those of you that are in pain are going to be free today. Once I rebuke it and it leaves you, you cannot allow it to come back. If he tries to come back, you kick him out again! Don't entertain any other thoughts. Don't allow any fiery darts to tell you you've got anything else. Once the pain goes, it's gone! Don't go looking for some disease. Don't go searching for a name to put on it. *You know the Name* and the name of Jesus is above every one of those names!

> *The name of Jesus is above every one of those names!*

Right now, in Jesus' name, I speak to you. Loose! Loose them! Now, right where you are, put this book down and begin to move your body. Check it. Don't look for the pain. Look for the miracle.

*If the Holy Spirit can come on a virgin
and impregnate her with a real baby,
then how difficult is it for God
to meet your need?*

Chapter 13

Impregnated by Desire

And in the sixth month the angel Gabriel was sent from God unto a city of Galilee, named Nazareth, To a virgin espoused to a man whose name was Joseph, of the house of David; and the virgin's name was Mary. And the angel came in unto her, and said, Hail, thou that art highly favoured, the Lord is with thee: blessed art thou among women. And when she saw him, she was troubled at his saying, and cast in her

> mind what manner of salutation this should be. And the angel said unto her, Fear not, Mary: for thou hast found favour with God. And, behold, thou shalt conceive in thy womb, and bring forth a son, and shalt call his name JESUS. He shall be great, and shall be called the Son of the Highest: and the Lord God shall give unto him the throne of his father David: And he shall reign over the house of Jacob for ever; and of his kingdom there shall be no end. Then said Mary unto the angel, How shall this be, seeing I know not a man? And the angel answered and said unto her, The Holy Ghost shall come upon thee, and the power of the Highest shall overshadow thee: therefore also that holy thing which shall be born of thee shall be called the Son of God.

Luke 1:26-35

The angel came from God to give an assignment to a very privileged woman. I asked the Lord about this because I've personally had an encounter with an angel. I was terrified! I was in the shower, *naked*. When he appeared, I dropped to my feet on the shower floor. I wouldn't look at him. It wasn't a horror-film-type-fear, but it was the fear of God amidst this awesome presence that I felt. Every time angels appear in the Bible, people fall down. The angels have to stand them up and tell them to fear not. The presence of an angelic being is awesome!

The angel, Gabriel, was sent directly from God to give a message to a young girl. One time I asked the Lord, "How did you pick this woman? How did you pick this child?" He said to me, "Her heart drew Me to her."

> **Blessed are the pure in heart: for they shall see God.**
>
> Matthew 5:8

The Lord said, "Every time she heard the Scriptures preached in the synagogue about the Savior, inside her heart she said, *'Let it be me. Let me be the one. Oh God, if I could just be the one that carries the Savior of my people.'* When she heard the message of His coming, destiny rang like a bell within her heart. Somewhere deep within, the desire to carry the Savoir of the world was planted by the seed of the Word."

When she heard the message of His coming, destiny rang like a bell within her heart.

The angel came to the young girl and said, "Hail Mary thou that are highly favored. The Lord is with thee. Blessed art thou among women. And when she saw, she was troubled at his *saying*." She was not troubled that he was an angel! She was not troubled that he came to her. Somewhere inside she had an expectation.

God never comes *unless* we're willing to open the door. There was an expectation. She was ready. She had been prepared by some type of foreknowledge. Otherwise, she would have been totally caught off guard. She would have said, "*Who* are you, *what* are you and *why* are you here?" She didn't say that though! She stayed quiet. When the angel spoke to her, she was troubled because of *what he said*, not because of *who he was*. She was ready for her miracle. Somewhere deep down inside her heart, she had that place already prepared. She was ready to be used by God.

> *God never comes unless we're willing to open the door.*

Your miracle wants to come to you right now. You have a divine appointment. Throughout the course of these pages, God has been preparing you to receive the implantation of whatever you need. *He has gifts for you.*

Somewhere deep inside you said to God, "Oh I want to be healed. Oh, I want to be free. Oh, I want this thing to stop or that thing to stop or this thing to leave me alone. Oh, I want a change." God has heard your prayers. He has heard your heart's cry!

Just like Mary, your call has come up before the throne of God. Mary was chosen out of all the virgins in the land. Why her? Her heart cried, "Let it be me! Let me be the one!" Whatever you have longed for in the secret place of your heart, God will give it to you. The Lord will give you the desires of your heart right now. He will not refuse you.

Mary didn't argue with the angel. She didn't say, "I'm not the virgin." She just asked a very simple technical question: *How is this going to happen?* How is this miracle going to happen to me, seeing that I know not a man?

> *Just like Mary, your call has come up before the throne of God.*

"There's no natural way for it to happen! There's no natural way for my breakthrough to come to me right now! I can't see God, I can't see angels, I can't see breakthrough. Why should I believe that God has an appointment with me right now?"

Whatever you said in your heart has ascended to God. The pureness of that desire has opened your heart to heaven. In turn, heaven has been opened to you. God will give you the desires of your heart. You are at the right place at the right time. The power of the Most High shall overshadow you.

Delight yourself also in the Lord, And He shall give you the desires of your heart.

Ps. 37:4 NKJV

Never a wish in his *(her)* heart has thou disappointed, never a prayer on his *(her)* lips denied.

Ps. 21:2 KNOX

The Substance of God

I was in Hawaii in an extended revival service. We had been preaching for thirty days straight. I was exhausted. My physical body was tired. The people wanted to dance for two hours and I wanted to dance for two hours, *but my body didn't want to dance at all.*

I was standing on the front row and I said to the Holy Spirit, "I am wiped out! How am I going to do this tonight?" He replied, "I'm not tired at all."

Immediately, I went into a vision. I saw the cross, and I saw blood pouring from the cross. Blood covered multitudes of people. I asked Jesus what it was. He said, "That's the blood of God." I said, "What do you mean?" He said, "The blood that was in Jesus' veins when He was on the planet was *the heavenly substance of Father God made material.* That's the price that had to be paid for all mankind."

It was just the same when Jesus materialized in Mary's womb. The substance of God came down and made the strongest, most tangible weapon that God could make against the enemy. God's substance became material blood. God's substance became a baby in the womb of a virgin.

God's substance became a baby...

How much easier is it for the Holy Ghost to come upon you right now and for God to give you whatever you need? He is not a respecter of people. He loves you just as much as He loved Mary. The Lord wants to take the substance of heaven and materialize it in your life.

Be It unto Me, God

After the angel gave the word to Mary, he left. The Spirit of God came upon her, and a miracle materialized within her.

The Spirit of God is hovering over you, waiting to give you your heart's desire. He's waiting. You don't have to do anything to qualify for it. You just have to do what Mary did. She didn't understand, but some things you don't have to understand. You just have to believe. Mary said, "Be it unto me according to Your Word."

The Holy Ghost came upon Mary, and a physical child was implanted in her womb. A supernatural transaction took place between heaven and earth. If the Holy Spirit can come on a virgin, and impregnate her with a real baby, then how difficult is it for God to meet *your* need? If God can do that, I think He can do anything.

> *The Spirit of God is hovering over you, waiting to give you your heart's desire.*

There are two components to the miracle that is taking place in your life *right now*. You have to hear it, and then you have to believe it. Mary, the mother of Jesus, said, "Be it unto me, God, according to Thy will." God didn't give her a diagram. God didn't hand her a business proposal.

Allow the Lord to take His spiritual scalpel and open you up. Allow the blood of Christ to heal you. Allow the balm of Gilead to cover and erase your memories. What is happening to you? Like Mary, a supernatural transaction is taking place. The image of heaven is being implanted in your heart.

The image of Heaven is being implanted in your heart.

Women in the Body of Christ are going to rise up and take their place! It's not going to be the boy's club anymore. Watch out world, the daughters of God are coming! I'm not teaching from a place of feminism. I have an *amazing* marriage. My husband and I love one another. We are submitted one to another, but my husband has *never* held me down. He's never let anybody else hold me down either. He's never told me *what* to wear or *how* to act or *who* to be. He's never told me, "This is who Jesus is." He just let the Holy Ghost come upon me.

All you have to do is say, "Be it unto me according to Your Word." There are desires on the inside of your heart. On the inside you are crying, "Let it be me! Let it be me, Lord." Your miracle is here. Your destiny is at hand. This is your moment! Allow God to give you your heart's desire. Receive it by faith, just like Mary did. *Be it unto me God.*

"Well how can it happen so quickly?" It's supernatural! The Holy Ghost is performing a spiritual surgery in your life. He has His anesthetic on you. He is overshadowing you, and a supernatural transaction is taking place. Can it really be that easy? Oh, yes! I want you to put your hands on your spirit and begin to pray in the Holy Ghost right now. Just pray like I taught you earlier. Give birth to your destiny in the Spirit.

Pray into your miracle!

The Crown of Glory

Never forget who you are or why Jesus gave His life for you!

The LORD will hold you in his hands for all to see – a splendid crown in the hands of God.

Isaiah 62:3 NLT

Child of God, you are priceless! You are precious! You are a magnificent jewel in the hands of God! This is *your* hour to shine in the light of His glory. This is your time to stand and magnify His goodness! Rise up daughter of God! Heaven has prepared *you* for this hour. You are the hope of generations of women to come. Run the race! Press into destiny! You were born for this hour. Daughter of God, this is *your time* of triumph. Let them follow you as you follow Christ.

I love you.

*You may not have realized it
when you woke up this morning,
but all of heaven has been working
on your behalf to introduce you to
the miracle move of God!*

Epilogue

Reach For the Stars

...Perhaps you have come to royal dignity for just such a time as this.

Esther 4:14b NRSV

Child of God, this is only the beginning! There is no limit to your growth in God. You have been divinely summoned *for such a time as this*. The God who created you, the God who intimately knows you, has orchestrated this moment in your life. He has positioned you for promotion. Daughter of God, the sky is the limit!

> **God can do anything, you know - far more than you could ever imagine or guess or request in your wildest dreams! He does it not by pushing us around but by working within us, his Spirit *deeply* and *gently* within us.**
>
> Ephesians 3:20 The Message

This page marks the beginning of a journey that will thrill your heart and exceed your dreams. Together, we have walked through the first stages of your healing, but the healing doesn't end here. This is just the beginning. This is your launching pad into the desire of heaven for your life.

This page marks the beginning of a journey...

Like Esther was prepared for a great king, you have been prepared for God's royal purpose on this earth. With the help of the Holy Ghost, I want to launch you into the limitless expanse of God. I want to stir that place on the inside of you until the fullness of the gift of God breaks forth like the noonday sun. I don't want to leave you, but rather, I would like to continue with you into that place of *wholeness*. God has sent me to train you for greatness. A healed woman is a powerful woman. Together, we can reach for the stars and do exploits for God!

...but the people who know their God shall be strong, and carry out great exploits.

Daniel 11:32b

Men and women who have lived wisely and well will shine brilliantly, like the cloudless, star-strewn night skies. And those who put others on the right path to life will glow like stars forever.

Daniel 12: 3 The Message

The Healing Continues

Anxiety, stress, depression, suicide, eating disorders, Chronic fatigue syndrome, Fibromyalgia, sleep disturbances, mental health issues, menopausal symptoms, psychosomatic illnesses, emotional pain....

- Every 78 seconds a woman attempts suicide. Every 90 seconds she succeeds.
- 7 million women struggle with eating disorders. 20 percent of those waste away and die.
- 90 percent of those diagnosed with Fibromyalgia are women.
- 85 percent of those diagnosed with Chronic Fatigue Syndrome are women.
- 12.4 million women are affected by depressive disorders.
- Worldwide, clinical depression affects twice as many women as men.

Go up to Gilead to get ointment, O virgin daughter of Egypt! But your many medicines will bring you no healing.

Jeremiah 46:11 NLT

Women are suffering around the world. Undiagnosable illnesses, phantom diseases and emotional torment relentlessly plague them. They try in vain to *pin the tail on the donkey*. No cure. No hope. No answers. Apparitions of torment haunt their lives. In desperation, they have searched the medical journals, analyzed case studies, devoured self-help books, taken herbal supplements, visited internet forums and run marathons... searching for a cure. Each turn yielded more questions and fewer reasons to hope.

Is there really an answer?

I don't want to leave you without the answer. I feel that I know you and throughout the course of this book, I believe that you've gotten to know me. I have opened my life to you, and now I'd like you to open your life to God in a brand new way. This is my mission.

> *I don't want to leave you without the answer.*

Do you believe that God has sent me to bring healing into your life? I have been commissioned by God to shine His light into every facet of your life. If you will continue on with me, I will show you the way out of the labyrinth of pain. You will rise to your calling. You will not be paralyzed by fear, fatigue, or depression. There is *healing* and *wholeness* for *whatever* is tormenting you. This isn't about a feel-good temporary fix. This isn't about a gimmick. I didn't write this book to give you *warm-fuzzies*. I wrote this book *specifically for you*, so that I could supernaturally walk you into your answer.

Am I coming on strong?

Yes. For your sake, I have to be. God has sent me to break you through the thing that has numbed you to destiny. My purpose and my passion is to set you free. A healed woman is a powerful woman. You have a God-ordained assignment on this earth. Only you can fulfill your purpose. As an eternal spirit, you will live forever, but your days in your *earth suit* are numbered. When you stand before Jesus in that brilliant city in the sky, He will ask you what you have done with the gifts He deposited within you.

> **God has given gifts to each of you from his great variety of spiritual gifts. Manage them well so that God's generosity can flow through you.**
>
> 1 Peter 4:10 NLT

Mobilizing the Army of God

Prescription pills, therapy, surgery, supplements, hypnosis, pain management, support groups, self-help books, biofeedback, wellness seminars, holistic healing…

The world searches for an answer.

Thank God for modern medicine, but the key to your supernatural transformation is training in the Word of God. God is raising up a spiritual army! Jesus is coming back quickly! The time is shorter than ever! As His coming approaches, God is mobilizing sons *and* daughters who will shine as lights in a world filled with darkness.

Today, the call of God has come to your heart. You may not have realized it when you woke up this morning, but all of heaven has been working on your behalf to introduce you to the miracle move of God! God wants *you* to walk triumphantly and to live supernaturally. He wants to use *your hands* to heal the sick, reach the lost, and magnify His glory with every facet of your life. *Remember*, a healed woman, is a powerful woman.

The eyes of the LORD search the whole earth in order to strengthen those whose hearts are fully committed to him…

2 Chronicles 16:9a The Message

The call of heaven has gone into all the world. God's eyes are roaming the earth, searching for hungry hearts that cry, *"Oh God, Let it be me! Let it be me!"* The daughters of the Kingdom are rising up to fulfill His end-time purpose in the earth. Are you ready to embrace His supernatural performance in your life? Are you willing to walk in the realm of miracles? Will you answer the call to be a miracle working woman? There has never been a time like this in human history. This is a day of divine opportunity. We are mobilizing the army of God.

Are you willing to walk in the realm of miracles?

Spirit Training

If you have experienced healing throughout the course of this book, I would like you to continue on with me into complete wholeness. Walk in my footsteps. Follow after me as I follow Christ. The key to wholeness is spirit training. Why am I so free? I am free because I committed myself to a spiritual training program.

God has supernaturally commissioned me and my husband to trigger and release the gift of God on the inside of you. He has given us the divine ability to impart what we are into you. If you will commit to on-going training, we will stir you into your destiny. We will teach you to walk in the high places.

I would like you to continue on with me into complete wholeness.

The tool that God gave us is a supernatural training program called International Miracle Institute (IMI). Why am I filled with peace? Why am I filled with power? I didn't start out this way. Through training, the revelation from the Word of God saturated me – *spirit, soul* and *body*. As I yielded to that power, the glory of God began to flow through me in ever increasing measures.

I am the first student of the International Miracle Institute. My husband taught me the keys to victory, peace, wholeness and power. While I was being delivered from years of abuse and torment, he would study the Word of God into the early hours of the morning. God would download revelation into my husband. In turn, my husband would teach me. Day after day he would train me in the things of God. Through the quickening power of the Word of God, my spirit became stronger and stronger. Wholeness and healing washed over me. The written Word became revelation, and that revelation ushered me into another realm in God.

What God did for me, He will do for you.

All Scripture is given by inspiration of God, and is profitable for doctrine, for reproof, for correction, for instruction in righteousness...

2 Timothy 3:16 NKJV

Ever Increasing Glory

The only answer is IMI. If you have experienced healing throughout the pages of this book, then take one step further and walk into wholeness. If you will trust me, *then continue on with me*. Follow in my example. Let me help you. IMI will lead you into the freedom you have longed for.

If this sounds like a method of brain washing, *it is*. Let the Word of God clean you. Allow revelation to wash over you. Give God the opportunity to sweep over you with the Word of His power.

> **Don't copy the behavior and customs of this world, but** *let God transform you* **into a** *new person* **by changing the way you** *think***. Then you will know what God wants you to do, and you will know how good and pleasing and perfect his will really is.**
>
> Romans 12:2 NLT

Your spirit is perfect. You spirit is alive to purpose and primed for power. It's the soul-realm that we're going to work on. The devil does not have access to your born again spirit. He can only shoot fiery darts on an unprotected soul. Your deliverance is in the transformation of your *mind, will* and *emotions*. As your mind is renewed, you will take up the shield of faith and extinguish *every* fiery dart.

> *If you will trust me, then continue on with me.*

God is strong, and *he wants you strong*. So take everything the Master has set out for you, well-made weapons of the best materials. And put them to use so you will be able to stand up to everything the Devil throws your way.

Ephesians 6:10b-11 The Message

IMI will arm you with the weapons you need to triumph over every circumstance. No longer will you be sucked into the suffocating undertow of defeat, but you will breathe free in the high places of God. You will ride the wave of strength and wholeness. Exhilaration will fill your heart like wind beneath an eagle's wings. You will run, walk and soar with ever increasing strength. Together, as an army, we will leave indelible footprints of glory upon the planet. Lives will be touched. Nations will be transformed. Victory will permeate the story of our lives. Follow me. Let's go places in God!

Dear brothers and sisters, pattern your lives after mine, and learn from those who follow our example.

Philippians 3:17 NLT

Through the power of God, we will mentor you and impart our lives into you. Whether you choose to train from a distance or train in person, we will help you. We will train you until your freedom is expressed in every increasing glory. Follow us as we follow Christ.

So, affectionately longing for you, we were well pleased to impart to you not only the gospel of God, but also our own lives, because you had become dear to us.

1 Thessalonians 2:8

On the pages following, you will have an opportunity to learn how you can continue on from healing into wholeness as one of our students. I have also included a card which you can mail back to me. Let me hear from you. Send us your picture! Write us and let us know that you are ready to train as a *miracle working woman* through the International Miracle Institute.

I love you.

International Miracle Institute (IMI)

Equipping A Generation Of Miracle-Workers!

The Lord has given Drs. Christian and Robin Harfouche a mandate to train and equip over 400,000 miracle-workers for the great end-time harvest of souls.

Through the integrity of the Word of God and the move of the Spirit, IMI is empowering a generation to live in victory and to walk in power.

Invest yourself in a supernatural training program.

Allow revelation from the Word of God and impartation from a major miracle ministry to supernaturally equip you for your end-time purpose!

IMI offers three training options!
IMI In-Residence Training (Pensacola, Florida)
IMI Correspondence Program
IMI Online

IMI Training at a Glance
Receive training by Drs. Christian and Robin Harfouche.
Grow in a practical revelatory understanding of the Word of God.
Learn how to have continual supernatural results in God.
Impact the world with signs, wonders and miracles following.
Fully accredited to confer earned undergraduate and graduate degrees.

International Miracle Institute
Correspondence Program
Training Curriculum

Year 1 Training Program

Heavenly Identity
Authority
God Man
Great Faith
Anointing
Miracles

Year 2 Training Program

Advanced Studies in Faith
The Supernatural
Healing in the Atonement
Ministry Gifts
Prophets and Prophecy
Demons and Demonology

For More Information:
Visit: www.globalrevival.com
E-mail: IMI@globalrevival.com
Phone: 850-439-6225

Dear Dr. Robin,

I would like to learn how I can continue with you from healing into wholeness. Please enroll me as a student in the International Miracle Institute. I am ready to train as a miracle working woman!

Please send me enrollment information for:

☐ IMI Correspondence Program
☐ IMI In-Residence Program
☐ IMI Online

Name _____

Address _____

City _____ State _____

Zip _____ County _____

Phone (_____) _____

E-mail _____

For more information:
International Miracle Institute
421 N. Palafox St.
Pensacola, FL 32501
Phone: 850-439-6225
E-mail: IMI@globalrevival.com

What does a *Miracle Working Woman* look like?

**Special Offer
$39**

**Miracle Working Women
Dr. Robin Harfouche**

Dr. Robin explores the lives of miracle working women who impacted millions and launched some of the great miracle ministries of the day. Learn how they overcame the persecution of being women in ministry and the practical faith application for miracle working women of today.

Regular Price $56
Purchase this powerful 8 CD series through this book offer for $39

For more information or a catalog please visit:
www.globalrevival.com
Global Revival Distribution
4317 North Palafox St., Pensacola, Florida 32505
E-mail: bookstore@globalrevival.com
Order Line: 850-439-9750

If you have enjoyed *Healing of the Female Spirit* we would like to recommend the following resources by
Dr. Robin Harfouche.

BOOKS
Healing of the Female Spirit Journal
From Hollywood To Heaven
Soul Ties
Agape Does Not Sleep With Phileo

AUDIO CD/TAPE SETS
Acting on God's Word
The Call Took Care of It All
The Final Harvest
Get Through The Wilderness
Angels
Steps to Becoming a Miracle Worker
Stuff You Need To Know About Sex
America On Fire
Holy Boldness
How Faith Comes
Practical Biblical Principles
Putting Your Faith To Work
Visions, Dreams, & Prophetic Insight
How to Get Rid of The Spirit of Greed & Anger
Miracle Working Women
Prayer: Communication With God
Spirit School

For more information or a catalog:
Global Revival Distribution
4317 North Palafox St., Pensacola, Florida 32505
E-mail: bookstore@globalrevival.com
Order Line: 850-439-9750
www.globalrevival.com

**Visit Dr. Robin's Women's Page
for a special message just for you!**

www.globalrevival.com/drrobin.html

For further information:

**Christian Harfouche Ministries
421 N. Palafox St.
Pensacola, FL 32501
850-439-6225**

www.globalrevival.com
info@globalrevival.com